DISSENTING OPINIONS

Feminist Explorations in Law and Society

Edited by
Regina Graycar

Sydney
ALLEN & UNWIN

First published in 1990
Allen & Unwin Australia Pty Ltd
8 Napier Street, North Sydney NSW 2059 Australia

National Library of Australia
Cataloguing-in-Publication entry:

Dissenting opinions: feminist explorations in law and society.
  Bibliography.
  Includes index.
  ISBN 0 04 442240 7.
  1. Sociological jurisprudence. 2. Women —Legal status, laws,
  etc. 3. Women—Social conditions. 4. Feminism. I. Graycar,
  Regina.

340. 115
Library of Congress Catalog Card Number: 90–082047

Set in 10/11pt Sabon by Graphicraft Typesetters Ltd,
Hong Kong
Printed in Malaysia by SRM Production Services

Contents

Acknowledgments

The idea for this book originated at the 1987 Australian Law and Society Conference. All the conference participants contributed to it through their enthusiasm for furthering understanding of the impact of feminism on legal issues, and the organising committee deserves special thanks.

I am particularly indebted to a number of people for their tireless work on the various tasks that go into turning a collection of exciting ideas and papers into a book. Thanks especially to Jenny Bargen, Bernadette Dattatreyan, Hester Eisenstein, Annette Hasche, Maria Giuffre, John Iremonger, Jenny Morgan, Malcolm Rodgers, Bronwen Tucker, the Faculty of Law at the University of New South Wales and Allen and Unwin.

Contributors

JUDITH ALLEN is senior lecturer in the Division of Humanities, Griffith University where she established and has directed the Women's Studies Programme since 1985. She is the author of *Sex and Secrets: Crimes involving Australian Women since 1880* (Melbourne: Oxford University Press, 1990) and her second book *Rose Scott: Vision and Revision in Australian Feminism 1880–1925* (Oxford University Press) is forthcoming.

REGINA GRAYCAR is a senior lecturer in law at the University of New South Wales. With Deena Shiff, she edited *Life Without Marriage: A Woman's Guide to the Law* (Sydney: Pluto Press, 1987) and with Jenny Morgan is currently completing a text, *The Hidden Gender of Law* (Federation Press). Her major research interests lie in the areas of feminist jurisprudence, legal education, family law and social security.

ADRIAN HOWE is a lecturer in criminology in the Legal Studies Department, La Trobe University. She is currently writing *The New Penology* for the book series: *The Sociology of Law and Crime: Feminist and Socialist Perspectives*, edited by Maureen Cain and Carol Smart. She has published in the areas of criminology, feminist legal theory, Australian feminist politics and American history.

MARI MATSUDA is a professor of law at the University of Hawaii, where she teaches civil rights, legal history, and torts. She has written on race, gender, and legal theory, and has lectured on these topics in Australia, Japan, and various parts of the United States. She is a member of the board of trustees of the US Law and Society Association, and is a participant in the Conference on Critical Legal Studies, and its flourishing affiliates, the Femcrits, and the Critical Race Theorists.

MARY JANE MOSSMAN is a professor at Osgoode Hall Law School of York University in Toronto, Canada. She teaches and writes about issues concerning women in law and legal education and is involved in a number of community activities supportive of women's rights. She was formerly a senior lecturer in law at the University of New South Wales.

CAROL SMART is a senior lecturer in sociology at the University of Warwick, UK. Her recent publications include *Feminism and the Power of Law* (London: Routledge, 1989) and *Child Custody and the Politics of Gender* (London: Routledge, 1989). She has worked in the field of feminism and law for several years and in 1990 was the inaugural holder of the Clara Brett Martin Chair at Osgoode Hall Law School, Toronto. She lives in Leamington Spa in Warwickshire, UK.

SOPHIE WATSON is a lecturer in the Department of Sociology at the University of Bristol, UK. She lived in Australia for nearly 5 years where she was a senior lecturer in the School of Town Planning at the University of New South Wales and acted as a consultant for the Australian Law Reform Commission. Her publications include *Accommodating Inequality: Gender and Housing* (Sydney: Allen & Unwin, 1988); *Housing and Homelessness: A Feminist Perspective* (London: Routledge and Kegan Paul, 1986); and *Playing the State: Australian Feminist Interventions* (Sydney: Allen & Unwin, 1990).

REGINA GRAYCAR

Introduction

The 1970s and 1980s have witnessed an extraordinary, and potentially revolutionary, proliferation of feminist scholarship. Feminist perspectives have transformed the academy in a range of disciplines, from the humanities and social sciences through to the physical sciences. It should therefore come as no surprise that legal doctrines and legal practices have also come under scrutiny from feminists. Law, and its related discipline, criminology, have been subjected to a range of theoretical and doctrinal challenges in recent years in an exciting array of new works informed and inspired by the insights of feminism. Indeed, so extensive has been the feminist critique of law that in some countries, for example Norway, feminist perspectives on law are now required components of all subjects in law schools (see Stang Dahl, 1986). In Australia, courses on feminist legal theory have become part of the established curricula of a number of law schools and gendered perspectives on what have formerly been seen as gender neutral areas of law are beginning to appear both in print and in law schools' curricula (see Graycar and Morgan, 1990).

Feminist critiques of law are particularly challenging for a number of reasons. First, at a basic political level, law is a central institution of state authority and a principal site for the exercise of power over all citizens. This is particularly significant since women, and in particular married women, were historically excluded from participation in the legal system, both through their lack of legal capacity and through their exclusion from the ranks of practising lawyers and judges (see Mary Jane Mossman's chapter 6 for a discussion of women's struggle to gain entry to the legal profession). Secondly, at a more theoretical level, the structure of law and legal reasoning has historically been seen to epitomise the values of rationality, neutrality and objectivity: the very values most challenged by feminist epistemological work which has exposed the male perspective inherent in the 'point-of-viewlessness' of purportedly value-free, neutral, objective scholarship (see, for example MacKinnon, 1983, 1987, 1989; Harding 1986, 1987). As one Canadian legal academic has put it: '"Men and the Law" is tolerable as an area of intellectual activity but not if it is masquerading as "People and the Law"'(Boyle, 1985: 430–1).

This collection contains work by lawyers, sociologists and historians. Its eclecticism demonstrates the centrality of legal regulation to the lives of women across many aspects of daily life. Yet despite this eclecticism, the contributors share a common concern with exposing the ways in which legal rules, practices, doctrines and policies have a fundamental impact on women's lives, an impact rarely acknowledged by the 'official story' through which accounts of legal regulation are so frequently filtered. The contributors, and many others, came together for the 1987 Australian Law and Society Conference, a conference broadly concerned with gender issues in law (see *Australian Feminist Studies*, No 6, 1988: 115–17). It was the widespread interest generated by that conference which led to the collection of the papers in this volume.

A critical issue for feminist political theory and practice in the 1990s is the meaning of 'equality' for women. Like motherhood, 'equality' is a value which can hardly be argued against at a rhetorical level. It is in the name of this value that liberal reforms such as anti-discrimination laws have been enacted over the recent period of renewed feminist activism. Some jurisdictions have gone further, passing laws aimed at affirmative action, or equal employment opportunity for women. But equality laws have hardly responded to the many and disparate forms of inequality experienced by women which are endemic to our society. Despite 'equal pay' in Australia, vast disparities still exist between the wages earned by women and men (see Women's Bureau, 1988). Completely excluded from the scope of equality laws are many other forms of harm to women: for example, the prevalence of rape and domestic violence has rarely been seen as a sex equality issue, despite the fact that these kinds of harm overwhelmingly happen to women and are overwhelmingly perpetrated by men (see MacKinnon, 1987, 1989).

It is ironic, then, that much of the recent wave of legal reforms has been directed toward removing the most overt forms of gender specificity from our laws in the name of gender equality. Gender neutrality has been liberalism's response to apparent gender inequalities: so we no longer have 'rape' on the statute books in NSW but rather the gender-neutral 'sexual assault' which can be committed by a 'person' against another 'person'. Another effect of recent liberal reform initiatives is that in their exclusive focus on the 'public' sphere of life (employment, accommodation, education and the provision of goods and services), anti-discrimination laws leave unregulated the private sphere of home and family, believed by many to be the principal site of women's oppression. This entrenches the apparent division between public and private, a critical area of feminist analysis (see O'Donovan, 1985; Pateman, 1983).

The authors in this collection eschew gender-neutral solutions and focus instead on the specificity of gender as essential to an understanding of important problems for women. So, for example, Carol Smart in chapter 1, 'Law's Truth/Women's Experience' demonstrates the dissonance between the gender-specific ways in which women experience the injury of rape and the divergent malestream constructions of women's sexuality which permeate the administration of rape law. She illustrates this most graphically with her description of the 'pornographic vignette' which, she argues, colours and ultimately constructs current legal understandings of women's sexuality.

Similarly, Mary Jane Mossman, in her historical analysis of women's struggle to participate in the legal system in chapter 6, draws out the connections between nineteenth and early twentieth century rationales for excluding women from the practice of law, and the current highly gendered notions of 'leadership' and 'merit' which are relied upon to limit the full participation of women. These are perhaps more insidious now than when women were much more overtly discriminated against.

Gender specificity is also central to chapter 2, Judith Allen's '"The Wild Ones": the disavowal of *Men* in criminology'. During the 1970s and 1980s, feminist criminologists focused on the exclusion of women from criminological study and undertook an array of work looking at the criminality of women and their treatment within the criminal justice system. This work illustrated how malestream models had claimed universality: first we had criminology, then we had feminist criminologies which demonstrated the absence of women from prior accounts. Allen's chapter has a different, but nonetheless equally gendered, focus: she looks at the absence of a discussion of the criminality of *men* and the inherently gendered nature of criminality. The attention given to women in recent feminist work, she argues, does not justify the absence of an emphasis on the maleness of criminality in conventional criminological work.

Adrian Howe, in her account in chapter 3 of the policing of young women, is bemused by the concerns of social control theorists about the net-widening effect of current regulatory practices and the concomitant increase in the 'penetration' of the state into the lives of its citizens. She highlights the different reality of young women who are policed in countless ways through and by constructions of their gender. In doing so, she documents the gender blindness of these social-control theorists and reintroduces a consideration of gender into questions about the control of young women who come under the scrutiny of state agencies.

Returning to the problem of the public/private distinction for women, Sophie Watson uses her feminist analysis of housing policies and practices in chapter 5 to comment upon recent reforms in the areas of family law and social security. She shows how government policies in these areas of critical importance to women are incoherent. Family law is, of course, left unregulated by 'equality' laws such as the Sex Discrimination Act 1984 (Cth) because, as suggested earlier, those laws focus on the 'public' world of the workplace and the market. And for reasons of government policy, the area of social security, which has a marked impact on the gendered constructions of women's financial dependence, is permanently exempted from the reach of the Sex Discrimination Act (see s.40(2)). This overt acknowledgement of the gender inequality in the social security system contrasts with other aspects of legal regulation of domestic life where inequalities between women and men are not so clearly conceded.

Custody law (see chapter 4, 'Equality Begins at Home') provides a good example. It has undergone significant historical shifts from the time when fathers had absolute rights to custody of their legitimate children, through to notions such as the 'tender years' presumption which relied on biologically determinist arguments to leave children with their mothers (so long as they were 'good' mothers), to the current reliance on the rhetoric of equality in child custody law and practice. One of the most interesting aspects of current debates around custody is the way in which conservative forces like fathers' rights groups have harnessed the rhetorical tools of liberal feminism to fight against what they see as 'discrimination against men'. From this position, it becomes increasingly important to unpack the multiple meanings of equality for women lest political campaigns by women become railroaded and redirected, with women as their targets.

Common themes emerge in each of these chapters, though their focus is on highly disparate topics. First, despite the major campaigns and resulting law reforms of the 1970s and 1980s, as we enter the 1990s, women remain subordinate to men in our society in a number of important ways which the feminism of the past two decades has not been able to change. Secondly, the oppression of women takes place in many areas of our public and private lives. Legal strategies that resort to ideals of equality and gender neutrality are imposed upon, and pay little regard to, an already established terrain of inequality. This entrenches and reinforces existing allocations of power. Any analysis of practices which regulate women must focus on the gender-specific nature of experience, whether that be a concern with women's knowledge and experience of the phenomenon of rape, or the fact that women overwhelmingly remain the carers of children. Gender blindness does not further our understanding of the relationship between women and men, and of the way that power and powerlessness characterise that relationship.

Finally, Mari Matsuda's eloquent chapter (chapter 7) provides a methodology for introducing not only gender but all other relevant differences between people into our understandings and analyses of human life. She calls for affirmative action of a different kind from that favoured by some of our governments: affirmative action in furthering our knowledge of the world. Since perhaps the most important contribution of feminist scholarship has been to expose the partiality of knowledges in every conceivable area of scholarship by the presentation of white malestream viewpoints as if they were 'universal', the only way in which to challenge that partiality is to require attention to 'outsider' perspectives. Matsuda provides an action plan for intellectual workers and suggests ways of ensuring that we take account of 'outsider' perspectives through such methods as book-buying quotas and other changes in our intellectual practices.

If the 1970s was the decade in which feminist activism forced questions about women onto the political agenda, the 1980s have shown the limits of liberal law reforms in responding to the subordination of women. The 1980s saw a heightened intellectual engagement with feminist concerns, with the development of epistemological challenges to academic discourse and scholarship. Through this growth in the sophistication of new ways of describing and understanding what we had always intuitively known about women's subordination, the failures of the equality and gender-neutrality models have become all too clear.

The challenge for the 1990s is to use these new insights to work toward a revised agenda for women. In the legal arena, laws proscribing discrimination on the ground of sex, which require a woman to show that she was treated differently from a man who is similarly situated, have done nothing to change how women and men become 'situated' in a gendered hierarchy. Nor, to use another legal example, has changing the label for the 'reasonable man' to the 'reasonable person' done anything other than to obscure the persistent maleness of the content of the standard. The essays in this book provide insights into legal regulatory practices which make clear what Catharine MacKinnon has called the question of 'who is doing what to whom'. Hopefully the continuing development of feminist scholarship in law will provide concrete new strategies for responding to women's oppression, shaped and informed by the important work of the last two decades.

1 Law's Truth / women's experience

This chapter examines three related issues. The first is the question of law's truth, or more correctly, law's claim to truth, which, it is argued, is part of law's power. The second is the nature and relevance of women's experience. The status of experience for knowledge and theory has long been contested and while there are certain problems with it, it ultimately provides a vital counterpoint to legal discourse. And, thirdly, there is the rape trial as an instance of the conflict between law's claim to truth and women's experience. I hope to provide a reason for retaining rape as a major area of contestation between feminism and law, in spite of the obvious limitations of law reform in this area.

LAW'S TRUTH

It might be useful to start with an anecdote. It tells a story which is quite common in legal circles. At a conference on family law in England, a discussion ensued on the problems of the existing system of split jurisdictions in which different levels of courts provide different and/or inferior remedies. Points were also raised about the dreadful conditions facing litigants: the lack of waiting rooms, the formal surroundings with their criminal justice overtones, the parties' lack of control over, and understanding of, the system. At this point a lawyer interjected, angrily dismissing our discussion as irrelevant nonsense. What really mattered in questions of disputed family matters,

The ideas in this chapter are drawn from a longer work entitled *Feminism and the Power of Law,* Routledge, London, 1989.

he maintained, was that the bench arrived at the 'correct' decision. The experience of going to law was irrelevant; even the differences between the jurisdictions mattered little. The only significant factor was that the final decision was the right one. Moreover, he claimed that he knew when a correct decision had been made and that any decent lawyer or judge knew this too. His thesis was that the resolution of conflict was a purely legal matter and that those who are legally trained need only to hand down the self-evidently correct decision.

He was uttering law's claim to Truth. His interjection was a simple and clear assertion that in any dispute (for example over who should have the custody of children, whether an ouster injunction should be issued in a case of domestic violence, etc) law has access to the correct decision. So long as legal reasoning is correctly applied to the facts, the correct answer will be forthcoming. Now, what is interesting about this story is not that a lawyer should mouth this well worn version of legal positivism, but that in public no one would dispute it. We know that legal positivism is not accepted uncritically any longer, but here it was an uncontested statement confirming law's status in a hierarchy of knowledge. What is interesting in this is not the issue of whether such proponents and defenders of legal positivism are deceived, are subject to false-consciousness or are instrumentally serving their own class, race or gender interests. Rather what needs to be considered is the power that law arrogates to itself by making this claim to Truth, or ultimate correctness. What is also important is how this claim can disqualify other discourses, confirming a hierarchy of knowledges in which law is positioned close to the top. Lay knowledge and women's experience does not count for much in this regime of Truth. It is to the question of the power that is generated by a claim to Truth that we should turn.

SOME INSIGHTS FROM FOUCAULT

Foucault had little to say about law in comparison with his more fully developed thesis on the development of modern, disciplinary society. His focus tended to be on how the growth of the human sciences, which he called the modern episteme, produced knowledges and new forms of power relations which engendered modes of disciplining that were no longer dependent upon the traditional methods of law (Cousins and Hussain, 1984; Couzens Hoy, 1986; Smart, 1985). In Foucault's terms, law is part of, or at least has its base in, the ancient regime that predates the modern episteme. Law is part of a different system of power, one that has been superseded by newer mechanisms of power, for example social work, personal regulation, rehabilitation and so on. Notwithstanding this shift, it is apparent that we still refer to the 'old' system and still think of power in terms of law, sanctions and negative control. As Taylor has argued,

> Foucault's thesis is that, while we have not ceased talking and thinking in terms of this model (i.e. power as a system of commands and obedience), we actually live in relations of power which are quite different, and which cannot be properly described in its terms. What is wielded through the modern technologies of control is something quite different, in that it is not concerned with law but with normalization (Taylor, 1986: 75).

For Foucault, law is part of a regime of power based on sovereignty in which it functions to allocate rights and to protect the power of the sovereign through the distribution of punishment and rights. So law is a kind of residue, but it remains a counterpoint to the newer mechanisms of discipline. Indeed, he argues that the social sciences were made possible by the conflict between these two regimes. He states:

> I believe that the process which has really rendered the discourse of the human sciences possible is the juxtaposition, the encounter between two lines of approach, two mechanisms, two absolutely heterogeneous types of discourse: on the one hand there is the re-organisation of rights that invests sovereignty, and on the other, the mechanics of the coercive forces whose exercise take a disciplinary form (Gordon, 1980: 107).

Law therefore still operates in the traditional way, but it is constantly challenged and undermined by the incursions of the 'psy' professions and the newer discourses of medicine and the social sciences. Hence Foucault looks at the shift in the treatment of law-breakers and the way in which we no longer speak of criminals but of offenders who need to be treated or rehabilitated. Similar shifts can also be witnessed in the field of family law where the rights of husbands and parents are yielding to non-legal notions of the 'welfare of children', and where welfare reports are called for whenever there is conflict over custody (see Smart and Sevenhuijsen, 1989).

It is argued then that there is a contest between law as a regime of rights and the newer mechanisms of discipline. Fundamental to this is Foucault's notion of power, which he has tried to separate from notions of law or prohibition. He sees power as positive, as technical and creative, rather than juridical or negative. Again fundamental to Foucault's analysis is the link between power, knowledge and truth. It is the question of truth which should be focused on here. By truth Foucault does not mean 'the ensemble of truths which are to be discovered and accepted'. On the contrary, Foucault uses it to refer to the ensemble of rules according to which the true and false are separated and specific effects of power attached to the true (Gordon, 1980: 132).

Foucault is not concerned with what is considered to be the usual quest of science, namely to uncover the truth. Rather, he is interested in discovering how certain discourses claim to speak the truth and thus can exercise power in a society that values this notion of truth. The exercise of power is in fact manifested in the claim to be a science because, in claiming scientificity, other knowledges are accorded less status, less value. Those knowledges which are called faith, experience, biography and so on, are ranked as lesser knowledges. They can exercise less influence; they are disqualified. Defining a field of knowledge as science is to claim that it speaks a truth which can be favourably compared to partial truths and untruths which epitomise non-scientific discourse.

Foucault does not compare the scientist's claim to truth, and hence exercise of power, with the lawyer's claim. Law does not fit into his discussion of science, knowledge and truth because he identifies it in relation to a regime of power that predates the growth of the human sciences. Yet there are very close parallels in terms of this 'claim to truth' and the effect of power that the claim creates. That is not to say that law attempts to call itself a science, but then it does not have to. Law has its own method, its own testing ground, its own specialised language and system of results. It may be a field of knowledge that has a lower status than those regarded as real sciences, but nonetheless it sets itself apart from other discourses in the same way that science does.

As an example of this, because of the encroachment of welfare principles into the domain of family law (for example the 'best interests of the child'), it has become necessary for law to differentiate itself from social work. It is vital for law that it does not simply become an arm of the welfare professions, with the bench merely voicing the distilled knowledge of what Foucault has called the 'psy' professions. In the same way, those with legal training are keen to separate and give higher value to their own skills than to those of lay people who are inside the legal system, for example lay magistrates and litigants. The following statements from interviews I carried out with solicitors in Sheffield in 1980 reveal clearly the hierarchy of knowledge that is presumed in law (Smart, 1984).

> At times I wish [the judge] would just take notice of the parties themselves and *do a lawyer's appraisal* of individuals, rather than at times, [taking notice of] in my book, inexperienced, undertrained operatives ... (that is, social workers).

4

(Referring to the influence of welfare reports)
I think that it depends a lot on the judge in the County Court. I think
the magistrates' courts are more influenced. I think that judges are used
to making up their minds on the *basis of the evidence* and what they
think about the parties before them, whereas the magistrates tend to be
less self-confident . . .

(Referring to lay magistrates in general)
. . . [Y]ou have to be a very expert practitioner before you can accurately predict which way [magistrates] are going to jump . . . [T]hey're
pretty fickle anyway, and they make decisions which don't appear to
be based on anything *normal.*

So law sets itself above other knowledges like psychology, sociology or common sense. It claims to have the method to establish the
truth of events. For example, the criminal trial, through the adversarial system, is thought to be a secure basis for findings of guilt and
innocence. Judges can come to correct legal decisions. The fact that
other judges in higher courts may overrule some decisions only goes
to prove that the system ultimately divines the correct view.

However law's claim to truth is not manifested so much in its
practice but rather in the ideal or image of law. In this sense it does
not matter that practitioners may fall short. If we take the analogy
of science, the claim to scientificity is a claim to exercise power. It
does not matter that experiments do not work or that medicine cannot find a cure for all ills. The point is that we accord such status
to scientific work that its truth outweighs other truths, indeed it
denies the possibility of others. We do not give quite such a status
to law, although we operate as if the legal system does dispense
justice, that is correct decisions, and we certainly give greater weight
to a judge's pronouncement of guilt than a defendant's proclamation
of innocence. The judge is held to be a man of wisdom, a man of
knowledge, not a mere technician who can ply his trade.

If we accept that law, like science, makes a claim to truth and that
this is indivisible from the exercise of power, we can see that law ex-
ercises power not simply in its material effects (judgments) but also
in its ability to disqualify other knowledges and experiences. Non-
legal knowledge is therefore suspect. Everyday experiences must be
translated into legal issues before they can be processed through the
legal system. For the system to run smoothly, whether it is criminal
or civil, the ideal is that all parties are legally represented and that
the parties say as little as possible. As a solicitor in a recent survey
of domestic jurisdictions stated, he tried to 'avoid the client speaking
in person—they tend to botch it up' (Murch et al., 1987). The point
is that the litigant may bring in issues which are not, in legal terms,

pertinent to the case, or they might inadvertently say something that has a legal significance unknown to them. So the legal process translates everyday experience into legal relevances. It excludes a great deal that might be relevant to the parties, and it makes its judgment on the scripted or tailored account (Cain, 1979). Of course parties are not always silenced, but even when they are allowed to speak, the way in which they are able to tell their stories, and how their experience is turned into something that law can digest and process, is a demonstration of the power of law to disqualify alternative accounts. This power is particularly problematic where rape is concerned as I shall show below. What, for example, is the legal status of a woman's 'NO' in a context where her experience is turned into legal relevances, where her evidence must then be corroborated and where she must in effect prove beyond all reasonable doubt that she did not consent?

There is, then, a dichotomy between what law may establish as truth and women's experience (and indeed men's experience, although the difference is not the same difference). Law constitutes a particularly alien terrain for women and it is important to develop this point further before turning to the complex issue of women's experience.

LAW AS ALIEN TERRAIN

If we ignore for a moment the divisions of law such as criminal, commercial, family, civil, public which law itself creates, we can regroup laws according to the realities of women's lives (see Stang Dahl, 1987). The laws which affect women most cross existing divides and, as Stang Dahl has pointed out, are more likely to be in the area of administrative regulation than in high status terrains like adversarial proceedings and High Court decision-making. The forms of law which are particularly relevant might include health law; regulations governing childbirth, pregnancy and abortion; social security legislation governing benefits like child benefit (family allowance), maternity benefit and income support; family law which concerns divorce, custody, maintenance, and so on. So far as the criminal law is concerned, it affects women most in relation to matters like rape, sexual abuse or social security frauds. These are all areas which can be located in the private sphere. Even employment law, which falls outside this sphere, can be seen as related to the private in as much as the regulations most affecting women are often to do with maternity leave, unfair dismissal (frequently arising from sexual harassment) or health and safety relating particularly to women's reproductive capacities. This is not, of course, the whole story of

6

women's contact with law, but where women resort to law, their status is always already imbued with specific meaning arising out of their gender. They go to law as mothers, wives, sexual objects, pregnant women, deserted mothers, single mothers and so on. They are not simply women (as distinct from men), and they are most definitely not ungendered persons. In going to law, women carry with them cultural meanings about pregnancy, heterosexuality, sexual bodies, vulnerable or vindictive mothers and so on. To put it another way, laws that deal with the private sphere operate on fully gendered subjects. Not only is sexual difference part of the very formulation of legislation, nor do understandings of sexual difference simply inform every stage of implementation, but women who enter the terrain do so as gendered bodies imbued with cultural meanings which often remain quite unstated. It is not my contention that law should be gender blind, but rather I wish to stress that where women contact law—in areas of life most significant to them —they are identified as gendered subjects, but the gendering is achieved through a prism of law (and law's claim to truth) *and* phallogocentrism.

PHALLOGOCENTRISM

Phallogocentrism is a neologism constructed from phallocentric and logocentric. It has been developed by French feminists, particularly those influenced by psychoanalysis (Duchen, 1986). It is not, however, necessary to take on board the full rigours of the post-Lacanian feminist psychoanalytic school to see how this term might provide some insights into a feminist analysis of law. While there are most certainly limitations to the value of this neologism it is worth experimenting with because it is one of the few concepts which may enable us to move away from superficial notions like prejudice, sexism and misogyny which oversimplify and provide a very one-dimensional view of gender relations. By one-dimensional view I mean those accounts which explain women's oppression in terms of attitudes, which simply need to be changed, or economic interests, which a 'class' action could defeat, or in terms of hatred, which identifies women who relate to men as relating to the enemy. It is not that these accounts have nothing to offer, but rather that feminism has begun to reveal the multifaceted nature of gender oppression. It reveals that gender difference, and hence oppression, exists in the language we use; it shows that the way knowledge is constructed is gendered; it suggests that sexual desire is not a matter of false consciousness but a deep psychic process which cannot be undone easily. Terms like sexism and prejudice provide a surface description of acts of oppression, but they do not begin to tap the meaning of being a woman or being Black in a culture which is oriented around white masculinity. It might be useful to look separately at the concepts of logocentrism and phallocentrism before considering their value to this debate.

Logocentrism

Logos means literally the father's spoken word. It is used to invoke a system of thought or ideas which cannot be said to be neutral, but rather is constructed under conditions of patriarchy. The term also embraces the notion of a binary system of thought. Accordingly, it refers to the way in which we construct understanding through the operation of opposites. Hence active only has meaning in relation to passive, truth in relation to untruth, culture to nature, rationality to emotionality, man to woman. The point is, however, that these binary opposites are not of equal value: one is subordinate to the other and that one is associated with the female or feminine. So terms like masculine and feminine are not mere descriptions of gendered attributes or differences, but rather convey a hierarchy of attributes and differences. The association between feminine, passivity, untruth, emotionality, nature is particularly manifest in the area of rape. Take for example the following statements from English judges:

> It is well known that women in particular and small boys are liable to be untruthful and invent stories (1976).

> Women who say no do not always mean no. It is not just a question of saying no, it is a question of how she says it, how she shows and makes it clear. If she doesn't want it she only has to keep her legs shut and she would not get it without force and there would be marks of force being used (1982).

> Human experience has shown that girls and women do sometimes tell an entirely false story which is very easy to fabricate but extremely difficult to refute. Such stories are fabricated for all sorts of reasons, which I need not now enumerate, and sometimes for no reason at all (1968).
> (Patullo, 1983)

The feminist use of the term logocentric therefore implies that, within the binary system of thought, reference to the feminine or female brings with it associations with less desirable attributes. Judges reflect this in their statements and law reflects it in its requirements (for example, for corroboration of a woman's evidence in rape cases; the requirement that two doctors approve a termination request by a woman). However, judges do not have to make obviously disparaging comments to invoke the negative meanings associated with all things female. There is an implicit, separate standard which is invoked in the most mundane and commonplace language.

Phallocentrism

Phallocentric is a term which is more familiar in feminist literature and is deployed to refer to a culture which is structured to meet the needs of the masculine imperative. However, it is a term which is meant to imply more than the surface appearance of male dominance and to invoke the subconscious and questions of desire and sexuality. The term phallocentric attempts to give some insight into how patriarchy is part of women's (as well as men's) subconscious, not merely a system imposed from outside and kept in place by threat and force. It attempts to resolve the question of why women collude in their own subjugation, why women as well as men undervalue the feminine (in both men and women) and give priority to the masculine.

This has particular significance in understanding sexuality and desire. Briefly, in spite of feminist challenges to the sexual status quo, sexuality is comprehended as the pleasures of the phallus. As Campbell (1980) has argued, the penis is constructed as the organising principle of the sex act. Female pleasure remains a mystery. One has only to consider the debate starting with Freud and continuing into the 1970s about the mystery of the site of female orgasm, and whether it should be situated in one place or another (Koedt, 1970). Female sexual pleasure is, it would seem, largely incomprehensible in a phallocentric world. Usually, however, it is presumed to coincide with the pleasure of penetration and intercourse. Whilst this may indeed be a form of pleasure, the mistake which is too easily made is to assume that penetration, being pleasurable to men, must always be pleasurable to women. Or, even if it is not assumed that it must always be pleasurable, the presumption in favour of the pleasure/intercourse linkage makes it virtually impossible for women to establish that it was not pleasurable when there is a contested account such as in the rape trial.

Because women's sexual pleasure is constructed as mysterious, as something that women themselves do not really know (that is, the 'frigid woman': see Cott, 1979) whilst men's sexuality is constructed around the supposedly more straightforward and obvious imperative of erection, penetration and ejaculation, women are often understood to be guardians of what men most want, but in which they place little store themselves. This in turn constructs sexual encounters or relationships in terms of how men can gain control of, or more access to, their pleasure which is inconveniently located in women's bodies. Figuratively speaking, women are seen as having charge of something which is of greater value to men than to themselves. Moreover, as men cannot ever really know when they give pleasure to women, they can really only hope to please themselves. This forms the basis of 'consensual' heterosexual relations *and* rape in a phallocentric culture.

The limits of the concept

Phallogocentrism, then, is a neologism constructed from the terms logocentric and phallocentric. The value of this term is that it conveys the deep structure of the meaning of sexual difference. It conveys that the way we think and the way we desire cannot be separated from the cultural meanings attributed to gender difference. But these meanings are not simply imposed upon us. We continuously reconstruct them to make sense of the world, and they explain, validate and create our experiences.

It is not men as a biological category who simply make the meanings for women, nor men's experience which always already defines women —although in some instances it might. Masculinity is constructed by these meanings as well as constructing them. However, this construction occurs under conditions of patriarchy (and capitalism and imperialism). In other words, masculinity is prioritised, and the exercise of power—no matter that it takes various forms—is gendered. It is therefore important for feminist theory to go beyond analyses of law which stop at the point of recognition that men, as a biological category, rule the law and that women are oppressed by it. Whilst this basic insight is valid to a point, it does not go far enough.

The concept of phallogocentrism allows us to go beyond superficial notions of discrimination or inequality to understand how the construction of femininity and masculinity, and the values attributed to these constructs, are part of our world view and identity. They are also part of law. Hence notions like sexual inequality or equal treatment, which *might* have some political purchase in areas like employment law, are profoundly problematic in that they look only to surface differences, that is those measured by wage packets or job promotions. Whilst these things are important to the material conditions of women's lives, it is now quite apparent that equal pay or anti-discrimination legislation hardly touches the surface of the problem of women's poverty (Gregory, 1988). The deeper problem remains unscathed. In areas such as rape and also sexual abuse, pornography or child custody, the concepts of discrimination and inequality have even less purchase.

The concept of phallogocentrism is, however, not without its limitations. Basically the identification of a system of knowledge and

10

logic based on binary meanings does not help us to go beyond this form of conceptualisation. It identifies that language is not a neutral field and that a level of negative or positive meanings is always already located in the words that we use. But it would seem to be, a priori, beyond our imagination to get outside this logos. It is hard, if not impossible, to imagine a system of knowledge constructed outside conditions of patriarchy if all societies are in some sense patriarchal. The same problems arise with the concept of the phallocentric. Identifying the problem of the hegemony of heterosexist masculinity is one thing; constructing another culture with a different orientation is another. Yet some feminists do perceive solutions to these problems so it is important to consider them here, albeit briefly.

The French feminist psychoanalytic school argues that there is a stage in psychic development before children enter into the patriarchal symbolic order system of meanings (Duchen, 1986). This is the pre-Oedipal stage, which is argued to be pre-patriarchal in that the values of phallogocentrism have not entered into the psyche. In particular, little girls have not been initiated into a rejection of womanhood and an envy of the symbolic (or real) power of the penis. It is thus argued that, with the use of the psychoanalytic technique, it is possible to reach back and retrieve this uncontaminated phase. Psychoanalysis provides the method for reaching back into early childhood experience and reconstructing the adult woman according to non-patriarchal tenets. This is a compelling argument, but only if the basic tenets of psychoanalysis are accepted. Without a certainty about the importance of the Oedipal phase, and without the assurance that the process of incorporation into a patriarchal culture occurs at this moment in a child's development, this solution is of doubtful value.

Other feminists, most notably Catharine MacKinnon (1983, 1987) and Kathleen Lahey (1985), have argued that the method that is required is that of consciousness-raising. Dispensing with the idea of psychoanalysis, they tend to argue that it is possible to reach an essential or pre-patriarchal woman through the process of collectivising women's experience. It is argued that a different reality, or a different definition of reality, is reached when women come together to express their experiences. Whilst this is undoubtedly the case, the problem is whether consciousness-raising generates an essential Truth about women's experience which is universal in its application. The question which must be posed is whether consciousness-raising produces the 'first principles' (Matsuda, 1986) of feminist knowledge, or whether it taps into a precultural, uncontaminated essence which is self-evidently true for all women. The more the assertion is made that consciousness-raising is a means to an alternative truth rather than a politics of knowledge, the more it sounds like the psychoanalytic view which seeks to find True Womanhood. Thus even though authors like MacKinnon recognise the limitations of treating all women as a unitary, homogeneous category, there remains the problem of invoking a collectivised Woman as an epistemological device to make transcendent knowledge claims.

The problem of the concept of phallogocentrism, therefore, is that it engenders responses which tend to invoke an essentialism in order to overcome the identified cultural components of women's oppression. If women enter into patriarchy as they enter into culture, it is hardly surprising that one seeks out the precultural woman who is a *real* woman, not a man-made woman. If the feminine has been constantly undervalued in the system of knowledge (the logos), it is hardly surprising that feminists attempt to give it a new value. However, there are dilemmas to be faced in going down this path. The central problem is that before one begins to celebrate the feminine, one must be sure that this is not the femininity constructed for women by patriarchy. MacKinnon (1987) has identified precisely this issue in her critique of Gilligan (1982). Gilligan has attempted to construct an alternative moral ethic based on feminine values. She calls this the ethic of caring and it is based on her argument that women speak with a different voice to men on matters of morality, justice and ethics. But MacKinnon argues:

> [Gilligan] achieves for moral reasoning what the special protection rule achieves in law: the affirmative rather than the negative valuation of that which has accurately distinguished women from men, by making it seem as though those attributes, with their consequences, really are somehow ours, rather than what male supremacy has attributed to us for its own use. For women to affirm difference, when difference means dominance, as it does with gender, means to affirm the qualities and characteristics of powerlessness . . . I do not think that the way women reason morally is morality 'in a different voice'. I think it is morality in a higher register, in the feminine voice (MacKinnon, 1987: 38–9).

We cannot therefore celebrate women until we know that they are real women. Hence we must develop the methodology for discovering real women and circumventing patriarchy. This returns us to the issue of whether to select psychoanalysis or consciousness-raising as our methodology.

I shall concentrate on the issue of consciousness-raising. The basic question to be addressed is whether consciousness-raising is a route to an inalienable standard of womanhood that is an alternative truth, or whether it produces first principles which can develop only by recognising the differences between women, and that the experiences of Black women or women of colour will not reveal the same truths as those of white women.

WOMEN'S EXPERIENCE: TRUTH OR FIRST PRINCIPLES

My basic argument is that consciousness-raising is a vital starting point to challenge dominant discourses which are oppressive of women. But consciousness-raising is a starting point not a finishing post. The resort to an essentialist notion of woman, which is implicit in the work of some radical feminists such as MacKinnon and cultural feminists such as Gilligan, I find problematic. Nor do I accept that the collectivisation of women's experience constitutes a truth against which all women's experience/knowledge must be judged. Rather, I understand consciousness-raising as producing competing accounts, the value of which lies in a political orientation rather than a claim to truth. The concept of women's experience is, therefore, not redundant. However, it is important that it does not become a fixed standard, or an inflexible notion that excludes women whose cultural background or personal biographies furnish them with very different meanings and experiences. To some extent, to invoke a notion of women's experience is political rather than epistemological. Its aim is to assert difference between, for example, law's definition of events, or 'common sense's' definition of events; not because any of these are the absolute truth, but because they are alternative discourses/accounts which have been silenced by the heavy weight of rational logic, legal logic, common sense and so on.

The point is, therefore, to retain the critical power of women's experiences at the level of challenging legal discourse. Mari Matsuda (1988) has argued that it is vital that legal knowledge and the legal construction of ideas about the world should be challenged by 'outsiders' knowledge'. She includes Black people as well as women in the category of outsiders, so her notion is broader than simply a gender divide. She acknowledges that there are many different voices, not just one, and that law is deaf to them all. If we add to this the recognition that law, as a discursive field, provides important ways of giving meaning to the world and of organising social institutions and processes, it becomes clear how important it is to tackle the content of this discourse (see Weedon, 1987). It also becomes important to challenge law's claim to truth which is linked to the exercise of legal powers. Arguably this should be approached less through setting up alternative hierarchies of Truth, which may in turn exclude other outsiders, and more by deconstructing this mode of exercising power.

THE INSTANCE OF THE RAPE TRIAL

The rape trial does not typify law's treatment of women, therefore every contact between women and law cannot be reduced to this one instance. However, the rape trial is a clear example of law's power to disqualify alternative discourses or accounts. It is perhaps the clearest example of the division between law's truth and women's experience and the way in which outsiders' voices cannot be heard.

The central concerns of the rape trial are consent and pleasure. Although the law is framed around mens rea and consent, the issue of mens rea only becomes relevant if consent/pleasure cannot be established. The man's intentions are therefore not a priority, but rather the whole focus is on the woman, her intentions and her pleasure.

Consent

Feminists have already established the centrality of consent to the rape trial (see Clark and Lewis, 1977; Adler, 1987). Not only has it been shown that the issue of consent transforms the trial from a judgment of men to a judgment of women, but it has also been argued that the consent/non-consent dichotomy is too narrow to allow for the expression of women's experience which may be the experience of submission. This is an important distinction. In seeking to find innocence or guilt, the law cannot accommodate the supposed ambiguity of a submission to a sexual assault. Either a woman does not consent or she consents. If the former cannot be established, the latter must have occurred. Hence, in law's domain the more that non-consent can be made to look like submission, the more it will be treated like consent. This typifies the way in which law cannot allow the complex nature of women's experience to enter into consideration. It clouds the issue, and it also shifts the power of definition too far away from the masculine imperative. So long as rape depends centrally upon women being able to prove effectively, beyond all reasonable doubt, that they did not consent, women will be faced with the problem of the logos. I mean by this that while what is feminine is always already on the negative side of Cartesian logic, she has a long way to go to establish that she is worthy while the masculine element is not.

It is important also to consider the sexual map onto which the idea of a woman's consent or non-consent is projected. I have argued above that in a phallocentric culture women's sexuality becomes mysterious—to themselves, it is argued, as much as to men. Women's rejection of sex is therefore always already ambiguous. Submission is already a part of 'normal' heterosexual relations. So what does it mean in cases of rape?

14

Take the following statement from an English judge in 1982.

It is the height of imprudence for any girl to hitch-hike at night. That is plain, it isn't really worth stating. She is in the true sense asking for it (Patullo, 1983).

How is it that for a woman to say Yes to a lift is to say Yes to something completely different, that is to sex? Why, having said yes to one thing, is it yes to everything? What are the linkages at work that lead us to doubt that a woman ever having had intercourse with a man could ever say No to him? Furthermore if it is common sense that women are mendacious in sexual matters, how can individual women establish the validity of their accounts of rape?

Pleasure

The rape trial is not simply an issue of truths and untruths. There are layers of meaning which will have a different significance under different circumstances. This brings us to the problem of pleasure. It is vital that a woman who has been raped should establish that she did not enjoy the abuse. If there is any suggestion of pleasure, the issue of consent is immaterial. No matter what violence may have been used to secure submission, a suggestion of pleasure erases the possibility of non-consent. There is no obvious calculus between the pleasure and violence either. While it might be expected that the greater the violence the more it could be assumed that there was no consent, instead the spectre of pleasure can negate the violence if it can be suggested that it is the violence that pleases. So the presumed pleasure of the woman can operate to exonerate the responsibility of the rapist. Take the following extract from a rape trial.

Prosecution Counsel: And you say she consented?

Defendant: I didn't say she consented, or that she didn't.

PC: Did she agree?

D: She didn't agree.

PC: Having said no at first, she just gave in?

D: She enjoyed it.

Judge: The enjoyment wiped out her initial resistance—is that what you are saying?

D: Yes.

(Adler, 1987: 10)

The suggestion of her pleasure erases his responsibility. But how do we, or a jury, know when a woman has experienced pleasure? How can we believe a woman when she denies pleasure? If women's orgasm eluded scientific study for decades, if women are deemed to get pleasure through pleasing men, then how can we ever know beyond a reasonable doubt that no pleasure was derived?

Women's denial of pleasure can of course be sustained under certain circumstances. A middle-class white woman may be able to sustain this assertion if raped by a black working-class youth—but in such instances it is not gender that determines the outcome so much as race and class. Yet this does not mean that a woman's pleasure is not always a legitimate debating point. The following case is an example of the extent to which few women can hope to escape the accusation of pleasure.

In the early 1980s in a Northern English city, a young middle-class woman was raped by an escaped prisoner who had just murdered her parents in another room in her home. The barrister defending the accused argued that the young woman was known to like 'a bit of rough', that she frequented pubs where working-class men went, and that she had invited him into her parents' home. The barrister was being a good lawyer. He focused on the points which he knew would raise doubts in the jury's minds. The accused man was ultimately convicted of murder and rape. However, this case and others like it must draw our attention to the way in which consent and pleasure may no longer simply be attributable to certain categories of women, such as working-class or Black women. Pleasure has been psychiatrised. This means that what is most unlikely may be transformed into an individual's particular perversion. Hence forced sex with a person under circumstances of extreme duress may be redefined as (perverted) pleasure instead of being taken as evidence that rape has occurred.

In a rape trial, a woman's denial of pleasure must be taken in the context of layers of cultural contradictions over what this pleasure might be. Her denial of consent must be taken in the context of a woman's No meaning Yes. But the trial itself adds another dimension to this process. The trial procedures themselves construct the rape as a pornographic vignette. This constitutes a further, more invisible dimension to the manner of judgment of the raped woman.

The pornographic vignette

The more an account of rape has resonances with the standard pornographic genre, the less it will be regarded as rape. There are a number of narrative conventions within pornography (Kuhn, 1985). One is the vignette in which the woman says no, but her resistance is overcome and she becomes sexually voracious. Another is the woman who is ready for sexual adventure, will take on lots of men, and even surprises men with how willing and forward she is. They, typically, think themselves extremely lucky and take their pleasure. Consider the following exchange:

Defence counsel: I suggest that you put a record on and started to dance around on your own. While you were doing that, the defendants sat down and opened three bottles of lager.

Victim: I put no music on and didn't dance.

DC: You were offered a lager with a glass—you just took the bottle. You continued dancing and drank it rather quickly.

V: No.

DC: You went on dancing and went up to one of the defendants and told him to get up and dance.

V: This is all being made up.

DC: He said he wasn't dancing. You grabbed him by the arm and pulled him to his feet. . . . You said you were a bad woman and ripped open your blouse. That's when various buttons fell off.

V: It's all lies.

DC: (Later) you told one of the defendants that you like him and asked where the bedroom was.

V: It's all lies.

DC: I suggest you said you were tired and wanted to relax.

(Adler, 1987: 110)

Here the woman is required to deny her involvement in what might be called a standard sexual fantasy. This is not simply the stuff of soft pornography but also of the down-market newspapers. These accounts are common currency. They are the imagined substance of *other people's* sex lives. The point is that the wide currency of the fantasy makes it plausible, just as the wide currency of the No which becomes a voracious Yes makes this equally plausible.

But the pornographic content of the rape trial consists of more than this. The focus of the trial is the woman's account of the event. In the extract above, the defence counsel constructs his version of events and he will obviously try to discredit any alternative account. But even the prosecution counsel requires the woman to tell her story, drawing upon what is defined as legally relevant. Yet what is the meaning of a woman talking in public of sexual intercourse, of sexual coercion, of the detail of where he or they put their hands and penises?

Anna Clark (1987) has studied the rape trial in English history and has argued that, in the eighteenth and nineteenth centuries, the mere fact that a woman could talk of rape disqualified her as the sort of woman who deserved to be protected by a law against rape. This is not quite the case today, yet the story that the woman must tell, whilst she appears 'in the flesh in court' (MacKinnon, 1987: 111), is the same story that gives pleasure in the tabloid newspaper or soft porn magazine. She cannot dissociate herself from her body, the body on which the assault was carried out. As MacKinnon has argued in relation to sexual harassment, for a woman to appear in person to complain of sexual abuse is to lose the sympathy of the court. This is because they can see her and sexualise her: indeed the requirement that she tell a sexual story makes it impossible not to see her body in that context. We cannot ignore that accounts of rape are sexually arousing—tabloid newspapers thrive on this fact. The woman telling the story of her rape, even in her own words and not those of the defence counsel, runs the risk of being sexually arousing.

The process of the rape trial can be described as a specific sexualisation of a woman's body which has already been sexualised within the confines of a phallocentric culture. Her body becomes literally saturated with sex. Some women may be able to resist this to some degree, for example the very old, but the majority cannot. It is particularly significant for Black women and women of colour who encounter a third dimension to this process of sexualisation. Being a Black or a native woman brings with it a racist encoding of the female body. If any woman can be transformed into the woman in pornography, the process is that much quicker and more inevitable for Black women. Added to existing dimensions of sexualisation are racist ideas about insatiable, immoral, sly, cunning and easy native women. The dimension of racism is not exhausted by the issue of intra-racial rape as in the example I used above. It is the Black woman who becomes quite literally unrapable so far as law is concerned, and the possibility that she might define her experience of sexual abuse differently is simply inconceivable.

The rape trial is a process of disqualification and celebration. It disqualifies women's experience of sexual abuse. This is more than saying that law takes women's No to be Yes, or that law is sexist. It is both of these; but the point is that the very spectacle of the woman's account and the pornographic narrative she must relate draws the rape trial firmly into the realms of uncertainty and doubt. The law exaggerates a common-sense understanding of women's sexuality. It allows it free reign and it constructs the story of the rape in a sexualised form. The sexualised woman can then be disqualified. But at the same time it celebrates so-called natural heterosexuality. Because it is concerned with consent and non-consent, the sexual pursuit of women which may lead to submission is defined as outside the law. Being a sexual predator is regarded as normal, even desirable, for men. Sexualising all women is equally regarded as natural; pressing a woman until she submits is regarded as a natural, pleasurable phallocentric pastime. The rape trial will not allow for any critique of this 'natural' activity.

Women's experience therefore has no place in this process. Indeed it is hard to imagine how it could be brought in given that the problem extends beyond law and is not simply created by law. Yet the rape trial is a site of real conflict for women. It is not simply that the process of the trial disqualifies women's accounts, but the very goal of establishing a legal truth, that is innocence or guilt, undermines women's accounts. Because rape trials overwhelmingly rest on the question of consent, the finding of innocence is simultaneously the establishment of a legal truth that a rape did not take place. The man's innocence establishes the truth of women's mendacity. There was no rape. Of course many rapes are discounted long before they reach the trial stage (Chambers and Millar, 1983). The point is, however, that each acquittal and each complaint of rape that the police deem to be unfounded is, in effect, a proof of our commonsense understandings about women and female sexuality.

The rape trial epitomises the clash between law's Truth and women's experience. In the rape trial we can see how extensive is the chasm between the two. Yet the everyday reality is that the law's account of rape prevails. Moreover, because of law's position in the hierarchy of truths, it has the power to disqualify women's experience, not just publicly but individually for women themselves who are required to accept the law's account. In the case of rape, women do not simply encounter law as subjects who may suffer discrimination; rather, they encounter law as female bodies already imbued with cultural meanings. Their bodies are then subject to further sexualisation in the process of establishing legal truths. Women cannot easily escape their sexualised bodies nor the regime of truth which the law has the power to impose. Once we can understand this we can see that law reforms which, for example, seek to abolish the requirement for corroboration, or provide anonymity for complainants, while necessary, are far from being enough. Clearly questions arise as to whether we need an alternative criminal justice system to deal with rape, or even whether we should take rape out of criminal justice since it merely serves to disqualify women's experience. On the former, it appears useful to me to construct alternative ideas about justice and law (see, for example Stang Dahl, 1987). However, such developments seem impossibly far off and utopian in the Anglo/Australian context. The latter is simply unacceptable. Decriminalising rape would, ironically, only disqualify women's experience of abuse even more.

It would seem then that the struggle must be on the site of women's bodies. Feminism has already begun to challenge how women's bodies are defined and abused and it is on the level of providing alternative meanings to women's bodies that further work must be done. This may entail grounding ideas in women's experience of rape and what they find most unacceptable in the legal process, and turning these into demands for reform. But the demand for reform would not be a naive demand, namely one that expected the reform to 'work'. Rather the demand provides the opportunity to redefine women's bodies and women's experience and to challenge the hegemony of law's truth. The aim of introducing law reforms should not be to encourage or pressurise more women to subject themselves to the process of disqualification, but to provide a platform for discursive struggle. It is an important goal for feminism that it does not cede to law the very power that law can use so effectively to disqualify women. This means ultimately that we should not see in law the solution to a problem of which law itself is a major part.

2

'The Wild Ones': the disavowal of *Men* in criminology

The spectre of sex haunts criminology. The criminalities that this discipline presumes to theorise—criminalities created and revised by criminal laws—appear to be dominated by men. This preponderance as officially measured by policing, has increased during the past century (Allen, 1987a and 1988). Moreover, criminalities measured by other means, including victim and self-report studies, in many cases tend to confirm the official sex differential (Heidensohn, 1985: 143) even if disclosing rates of female criminalities higher than officially recorded (Campbell, 1981: 12; Morash, 1986: 49–53). Despite certain dissent, sex has been identified as consistently the strongest predictor of criminalisation and perhaps of 'criminal' activity itself (Harris, 1977: 13).

A century of criminology has comprised various schools of unitary, universalist theories of crime causation as well as some more specialised theories of particular criminalities. Capacity to explain the high sex ratio and sexed character of many criminal practices might then be posed as a litmus test for the viability of the discipline. Feminist criminologists, among others, have certainly thought so. They identify failure to theorise the basic sex specificities of criminalities as the greatest intellectual flaw in twentieth century criminology (Harris, 1977; Hindelang, 1979; Heidensohn, 1985). Some

This chapter was originally published in a slightly different form as 'Men, Crime and Criminology: Recasting the Questions' in (1989) 17 *International Journal of the Sociology of Law* 19.

feminists have worked to reform criminology to enlarge its explanatory prowess. Most typically this has involved attempts to construct a criminology of women—sex-specific theories of women's criminalities (Rosenblum, 1975; Scutt, 1976). Others have diagnosed the failure of criminology to adequately theorise the relationship between women and criminality as symptomatic of a terminal masculinism at the heart of the criminological project. In particular, they have criticised a criminology which, under the guise of universalism, turns out to be applicable only to men, ignoring, marginalising or failing in a comparable analysis of women. These feminist critics urge a relocation of feminist inquiry outside criminology (Heidensohn, 1985: 200).

In reply to feminist critiques of criminology, some critics renounce the pursuit of any unitary theories of crime causation—including sex-specific ones—as 'theoretically unsound and politically misguided' (Carlen et al., 1985: 6). In their view such theories can only propagate sexism, biological reductionism, essentialism, and humanism, as well as preserving the existence of the bankrupt discipline, criminology, and its problematic object of study, criminality (Cousins, 1980; Greenwood, 1981). Instead of searching for causes of crime, these critics hold that the more worthwhile project will be interrogation of how the system of criminal justice operates on specific populations. Importantly, this position rejects the representation of crime as masculine activity, preferring not to see criminalities as sexually positioned—at least not until, or unless, proven otherwise in specific instances (Carlen et al., 1985: 8).

Such a rejection of both the hitherto 'known facts' of criminalities —including their overall male dominance — and twenty years of feminist critique finds an interesting echo within a mainstream criminology otherwise determined to preserve itself intact. In the May 1987 issue of the *Journal of Research in Crime and Delinquency*, Smith and Paternoster condemned the feminist argument that general criminological theory is inapplicable to women. They contend that this judgement is premature. Moreover,

> [W]e regard this period of gender specific theoretical developments as the 'dark ages' of deviance theory ... the current call for a separate body of theory to explain the deviant conduct of women simply perpetuates the sterile, sexist origins of theories of deviance (Smith and Paternoster, 1987: 157).

The reformation urged here is one of sex neutrality. Indeed the mainstream journals have busied themselves publishing empirical studies 'proving' that no appreciable 'gender' differences exist in criminal and delinquent behaviour, against the century-old wisdom that crime has been a man's world. Hence, despite the feminist challenge, it is claimed that by more empirical work, general, universal criminology can be saved (Smith and Paternoster, 1987; Thornton and James, 1979; Canter, 1982; Figueira-McDonough and Selo, 1980; Silverman and Sinitz, 1974; Jensen and Raymond, 1976).

Initially, feminists might read this convergence of oppositions to sex-specific criminologies as old-fashioned misogyny, bad faith and anti-feminism. An objective of this chapter, however, is to explore the possibility that there is a serious issue at stake here for criminology *and* for feminism. It fundamentally concerns the placement of men as a sex within criminological theory throughout the history of the discipline, especially the categories constructed for dealing with sex specificities at particular moments in criminology's history. Arguably, it is the theoretical legacy of the discipline's failure to address the sex question in adequate terms that made feminist criminology an emergence to which 'there really was no alternative' (Heidensohn, 1985: 144). Yet feminist criminology has inherited certain liabilities whose origins are in the broader sociogenic framework of the discipline, as well as in some particular theoretical formulations of contemporary western feminism. These liabilities mar the acuteness of feminist interrogation of criminology as a masculinist knowledge formation—one with concrete effects on legal culture and criminal justice.

The argument advanced here is threefold. In the first place, in view of the central place of men in criminalities, criminology has never theorised its own sex question with regard to *men*. The only significant flirtation with theorising the category 'sex' for criminology were the handful of biogenic and psychogenic theorists attempting to explain *women's* low rates of criminality and non-criminality in terms of biological and related psychological endowments.

Second, the limited address of the place of men in criminality became possible for criminologists to consider only with the establishment of the sex/gender distinction, which worked to displace the focus from men and women to 'masculinity' and 'femininity'. This began in the 1940s with Talcott Parson's formulation 'sex roles' (Parsons, 1942), the precursor of the current sociological usage 'gender'. Arguably the analysis of criminalities through what is designated 'gender' in this criminological literature aborts serious interrogation of the sex question and consigns this work to arid descriptiveness. This argument can be sustained through the case study of the work of some of the more influential postwar, post-sex/gender distinction criminologists: Edwin H. Sutherland, founder of the differential association theory of crime; and Albert Cohen and Walter Miller, theorists of 'masculine' subcultural deviance.

Third, the position from which feminism would criticise postwar criminology's masculinism is itself predicated on the same sex/gender distinction that renders mainstream criminology incapable of confronting its own sex question. This will need to be examined and resolved in some way if feminists are to move on from the paradoxical position of seeming simultaneously to support the maintenance of a bankrupt discipline on the one hand, and on the other, to be cast by that same discipline as the vandals and visigoths inaugurating a new dark age. In part this paradox may seem largely a problem of how feminist interventions are perceived by 'other' positions, and could be represented as not a problem *for* feminism at all. It is at least desirable, however, that feminists engaging within and adjacent to criminology consider repositioning the status of sex—the sexed body, and the possibility of understanding it in more cultural and psychical terms (Gross, 1986).

This will involve dispensing with the sex/gender distinction, the mind/body split and related dichotomous conceptions, as well as reorienting and reformulating the theoretical objectives they have hitherto served. Reconsideration of biology and of the sexed body as one of its manifestations given cultural meaning will be vital to this project.[1] Such efforts will extend the fortunes of feminist interrogations of masculinist knowledge formations beyond internal critique.

MASCULINIST RENDERINGS?

Any general theory of crime causation is confronted with the problem of explaining why men have constituted between 80 and 90 per cent of labelled offenders (Allen, 1987a; Heidensohn, 1985: 2–8). Sex was a major preoccupation of late nineteenth and early twentieth century biogenic and psychogenic criminology. Unless the sex difference could be explained, these theories could be undermined. For if causes of criminality could be laid at the door of evolutionary atavism and genetic mutation, why was crime not the equal resort of random men and women in any given population? Biogenic theorists like Lombroso sought explanation in the distinct biological features of women as a sex, as well as their psychological characteristics, as determined by biology (Lombroso and Ferraro, 1895). In other words, having formed a general theory, the variable of sex posed such a threat that universality was qualified by specification, not of both sexes, but one sex—woman—in order to save the general theory from extinction. Lombroso decided that criminogenic atavism, while as present in women as in men, was nonetheless checked from manifesting itself as criminality. The reason was that other biological characteristics overcame or rechannelled it in most women. Maternity, the passivity of the ovum (which led to piety, conservatism and conformity), generally overcame criminogenic atavism in women. Moreover, even where these other biological traits did not triumph over atavism, the option of prostitution and related sexual delinquency provided an expressive and, in Lombroso's culture, non-criminal outlet for it (Lombroso and Ferraro, 1895; Thomas, 1907, 1923).

These enquiries into the biological and psychological bases of female non-criminality did not lead biogenic and psychogenic criminologists to redefinitions of their projects that acknowledged that the principal objects of study were men. Instead, they wrote one kind of book expounding general, universal theories of crime causation, employing the general categories of 'offender', 'criminal' and 'prisoner', and a second kind studying the deviance of the sex that deviated from the general theory—women (Ellis, 1901). The female body was subjected to an intensive criminological gaze; the male body was evacuated, disallowed, disavowed (Gross, 1986: 135).

Subsequent proponents of liberal and sociological approaches to crime have judged such biogenic and psychogenic criminologies as 'intellectually inadequate and morally distasteful' (Smart, 1976: 36), though not in terms of their specific failure to theorise the sex, men. Such criminologists left little role for the professional criminologist beyond identifying born criminals and constructing their likely taxonomies. It is not therefore surprising that interwar and postwar criminologists sought to place their discipline into a firmly sociogenic framework by affiliating with sociology and avowedly rejecting, to varying degrees, wholly biogenic and psychogenic theories of crime causation.

Edwin Sutherland, dubbed 'the "dean" of American criminology' (Leonard, 1982: 92), laboured successfully in this sociogenic quest from 1921 until his death in 1950. He influenced a generation of criminologists, and had as working colleagues the major social scientists of the period, including Talcott Parsons and Alfred Kinsey, who were establishing new research and theories of the family and sexuality (Parsons, 1942, 1951; Kinsey et al., 1949; Kinsey, 1953). Sutherland's influential work makes a useful case study for the present enquiry because of the ways he developed across the period in his handling of two aspects of the sex question confronting any criminology: the sex differential in crime rates, and the sexed character of criminal behaviours. A reading of his work discloses the difficulties that sex posed for generalist, sociogenic criminology. It also reveals the part played by a masculinist perspective in compounding these difficulties.

(The use of 'masculinist' throughout this chapter recognises that an epistemological position dedicated to the maintenance of current sexual arrangements in the interests of men as a sex can be identified, and must be recognised as political: in the same senses that feminism is reckoned to be a political as well as an epistemological position. While feminism and masculinism may be counterparted, the former works for the destruction of the existing sexual order, the latter for its assertion and its maintenance.)[2]

Sutherland held that a single causal theory applicable to all criminal behaviour was both possible and desirable (Cohen et al., 1956: 3). He believed that all criminal behaviour was learnt—and learnt in groups and intimate relationships. Moreover, criminal behaviour might express needs, values and cultural traditions, but it could not be explained by them (Cohen et al., 1956: 38–9). Finally, a person's criminal propensities will be determined by the associations and opportunities afforded them by social organisation; and these same factors will influence the frequency, direction, priority and intensity of criminal behaviour (Cohen et al., 1956: 8–9).

For Sutherland, hereditarian theories of crime were invalid, because non-criminals had the same genetic make-up as criminals. For similar reasons, he opposed materialist accounts of crime, because all poor people did not resort to crime, and because crime in urban slums was constant, undergoing no significant increases during economic depressions and periods of sudden, local unemployment (Cohen et al., 1956: 15). Criminologists' presumptions that crime was solely working-class behaviour were, he believed, skewed, because class bias in favour of the middle class and other white-collar groups meant that their crimes were either undetected or disposed of outside criminal justice institutions. As a result, they remained untheorised by criminology. Thus, he argued that rates of conviction were a poor gauge of criminality (Cohen et al., 1956: 52–3).

In defining crime by non-legal rather than legal criteria, Sutherland sought to widen the address of criminology. He believed that crime was to be found in all social, occupational, cultural and spatially designated groups, stressing social structure and social group definitions in the genesis of criminal patterns and associations. These convictions made him equally an enemy of psychogenic explanations of crime as an individualised psychical resort, patterned from infancy (Cohen et al., 1956: 3, 26).

The sex variable in reported criminality and the sex-specific nature of criminal behaviours posed explanatory problems for Sutherland's theory of differential association. His theory had been expounded piecemeal until it was relatively complete by the end of the 1930s. Recognising the sex problem, he wrote:

> Perhaps there is nothing that is so frequently associated with criminal behaviour as being a male. But it is obvious that maleness does not explain criminal behaviour (Cohen et al., 1956: 19).

26

In this rejection of biogenic explanations, his argument strategy resembled that against other hereditarian and psychogenic explanations: for all men clearly did not become criminals. If he rejected the category sex as explaining male dominance, his work in the period 1921–1941 had offered no alternative explanation for this most striking 'fact' about criminality.

From the early 1940s, however, two emergences began to impinge on Sutherland. His theory was criticised as inapplicable to vast areas of criminality, especially interpersonal sex and violence offences, challenging him to demonstrate its force in explaining such behaviours (Cohen et al., 1956: 31). In addition, his colleague Talcott Parsons was attempting to theorise the relations and functions of the modern family. Parsons coined the term 'sex roles' in 1942. It was to presage the sociological use of the ancient term 'gender' (Gould and Kern-Daniels, 1977: 182). By 'sex roles', Parsons referred to the socially ascribed behaviours, attributes and capacities assigned to be appropriate for each sex. The sociological shorthand for this complex process became 'masculinity' and 'femininity'. Anthropologists like Margaret Mead had shown that the content of 'masculinity' and 'femininity' varied enormously from culture to culture (Mead, 1935). Despite the fact that nonetheless this 'gender' content was 'lived' in relation to male and female bodies within each respective culture (Gatens, 1983: 149–50), many western social scientists seized upon the lack of universality in the content of masculinity and femininity —gender—as grounds to exile biology (nature) once and for all from the framework of social enquiry. Biology could generally contribute nothing to sociology; and more specifically, biological sex identity need bear no necessary relation to socially assigned gender. The sexed body was rendered passive and neutral with regard to the formation of 'gender consciousness' (Gatens, 1983: 146). Hence, persons of either sex could exhibit measurable rates of masculinity and femininity. Moreover, their levels of 'gender' conformity were, by definition, variable, depending on 'social' inputs, later called 'socialisation'.

Critics have called this theoretical development the sex/gender distinction. It enlarged, even revolutionised, the claims of sociology by rendering key aspects of men's and women's attributes, capacities and behaviours amenable to sociogenic explanation and specification. At last, sociologists had something sociological to say about men and women (Grosz, 1987a: 1–2).

The implications of the sex/gender distinction inaugurated by Parsons' 'sex roles' for postwar criminology were momentous. Seeking to explain one of the most sexed of behaviours, anti-biogenic criminologists quickly began to reorient their work in the light of 'gender'.

By 1945, Sutherland was able to contend that boys are 80 per cent and girls 20 per cent of delinquents

> because parents and other intimate associates define one kind of propriety for girls and another for boys, and exercise one kind of supervision over girls and another for boys (Cohen et al., 1956: 33–4).

His theory seemed to accord with known fact, for while equal numbers of boys and girls inhabited poverty-stricken slums, it was the boys in general who turned to crime (Leonard, 1982: 110–11). Sutherland did not, however, push matters much further and attempt to account for what interests or social objectives might be at stake in these 'gender' differentiated 'definitions' and 'kinds of supervision'. His remarks here may describe, but they do not explain.

On the other hand, Sutherland's frequent discussion of sex-specific crimes is confined to demonstrating the applicability of his general theory of differential association to them, against the charges of his critics. With such examples as wife murder, incest and lesbianism, he attempted to save his theory. (In the process he disclosed certain of his assumptions and possibly anxieties about men, women and sexuality).

In the example of wife murder, he insisted that this occurs like any and all other crimes—men learn through associations with what he calls 'a criminal pattern', a definition of a situation in which it is appropriate to commit a particular crime. In 1944 he wrote that a man commits this crime, however,

> only when the situation defined as appropriate arises or can be located. Having learned through association with others that he should murder his wife if he catches her in an unfaithful relationship, he does so in accordance with the learned definition only when the occasion arises (Cohen et al., 1956: 34).

In a second example, that of incest, Sutherland notes that fathers who engage in this crime with their daughters

> are concentrated in the age group between forty and sixty and in families in which the mothers have died, are sick, or are for other reasons not available for legitimate sex relations (Cohen et al., 1956: 33).

To support this 'reading' he draws on analogy with male prisoners, who denied legitimate heterosexual access, frequently resort to homosexual relations (Cohen et al., 1956: 33). Differential association can still explain incest, since

> fathers whose wives are dead or sick often spend an increased portion of their spare time in low resorts where they may have more contact

with various forms of illicit sex behaviour and this may include contact with the pattern of incest (Cohen et al., 1956: 34).

A third example is Sutherland's use of a case of lesbianism to dramatise the process of criminal association and the factors which might lead the alternatives to criminality (in this case criminal perversion) to be overcome in any individual:

An isolated and unattractive girl was taken into friendship by another girl and was being gradually inducted into a homosexual relationship. In time the first girl became vaguely aware that the relationship was progressing beyond the conventional limits and became disturbed. She secured books on homosexuality and discovered with horror that the relationship was defined in the literature as the early stages of sex perversion. She went to the other girl with a firm determination to sever the relationship. But as she talked with the other girl and thought about it in more detail she was faced with two alternatives: isolation and loneliness without homosexuality; or a much desired intimate friendship that involved homosexuality. She chose the latter and became a confirmed homosexual not only because of her initial contact with that pattern but also because she could find no other way of satisfying the need for intimacy and friendship. If she had been an attractive and gregarious girl, she would presumably given the same contacts with the pattern of homosexuality, have severed this initial relationship without hesitation (Cohen et al., 1956: 35).

All of these examples are sex specific. Sutherland's attempts to apply a sex/gender distinction to their explanation—to locate them in the sociogenic terms of differential association—foundered, however, on certain assumptions and closures he applies, apparently unknowingly, which turn out to be biogenic or psychogenic in tenor, thus frustrating his theoretical objectives. Moreover, his focus on gender as the matter at stake in criminogenic association leads him to ignore aspects of the problem inseparable from an analysis of sex. For instance, in the case of wife murder, could the fact that the converse situation—of wives murdering unfaithful husbands—is comparatively rare generate further important questions that the theory of differential association would need to be able to answer? If Sutherland is correct that cultural endorsement exists for this kind of 'masculine' definition of a situation in which to kill, would he not need to enquire why this endorsement is offered to men and why it is unavailable to women faced with the same provocations? In other words, while he seems to be discussing men's options in wife murder, his failure to discuss the comparable situation of women in husband murder results in an inability for his theory to show why it is *men* who become the sole bearers of this masculine definition, why it is *men* who come into association with this gendered criminal pattern and not women? He shows no curiosity about what the equivalent feminine pattern might be in response to the unfaithful husband. In short, Sutherland not only offers mere description, but description that is partial and lopsided.

Meanwhile, Sutherland proceeds with decidedly biologicist understandings of the sexuality of the incestuous father, understandings that obstruct the full interrogation and comparison of men and women that his theory needed in order to convincingly establish its credentials. Mothers whose partners were dead or sick 'or for other reasons not available for legitimate sex relations' almost never resorted to incest according to then current studies of incest (Ward, 1984). Yet fathers, placed in the same situation, undertook low resorts, contacted illicit sex behaviour including the 'incest pattern', and, by the mechanics of the theory of differential association, with their anticriminogenic associations overcome, were propelled irresistibly toward their daughters. Sutherland needed to acknowledge and explain this sex difference in the pattern of incest. He does not, however, discuss incest in these terms. While only fathers are addressed, Sutherland does not say that incest is a 'masculine pattern'. By the same token, he does not enquire into the situation and behaviour of mothers living for various reasons in unchosen celibacy. Does Sutherland assume, and is the reader to assume, that only men would be expected to actively respond to unchosen celibacy with criminal incest? In the absence of other specification, it appears that Sutherland exhibits here an unexamined hydraulic and essentialist understanding of male sexuality. Historically this understanding requires, in the shadows, passive, receptive female sexuality. For him, it seems there were no questions to ask about women and incest. Paradoxically, he thereby explored nothing about *men* and incest.

Possibly the basis of this closure is exposed later in Sutherland's career when he became a tireless campaigner against sexual psychopath laws. To prove that women faced little appreciable danger from rapists, he contravened his own previous argument that conviction rates were an unsound measure of criminality and argued that the low conviction rates for rape afforded proof. Moreover, in radio talks, public speeches and published works, he authoritatively insisted the women charge men with forcible rape 'for the purpose of blackmail', 'to preserve their reputations' (after consenting intercourse) and that in any case rape is practically impossible 'unless the female has been rendered nearly unconscious by drugs or injury'. Finally, he asserted 'many cases reported as forcible rape have involved nothing more than passive resistance'! (Cohen et al., 1956: 187–8).

In Sutherland's account of the descent of the first girl into lesbianism, his evident homophobia and phallocentric inability to imagine lesbianism as a considered erotic choice and/or chosen sexual identity make him unable to apply successfully his sociogenic differential association theory. For in setting up the girl's options, he fails to escape the biogenic and psychogenic explanations he so despises. The unspoken assumption in his account is that if only she had been attractive (biogenic) and gregarious (psychogenic) she would be selected as a sexual partner by men, so that contact with the criminal pattern of lesbian perversion would have had little effect on her.

Sutherland's embrace of the sex/gender distinction as a means of rescuing pre-existing, sex-blind general theory of crime causation failed. Deployment of the category gender allowed him to describe aspects of the differentiated cultural existences and behaviours of the sexes, including their criminalities. Yet even thus revised and instanced with 'gender' specific examples, he had no sociogenic account of why the content of 'masculinity' and 'femininity' had been given the characteristics they had, nor why the definitions, patterns and associations that were typically feminine were so non-criminogenic. In other words, although he observed that crime was overwhelmingly and symbolically masculine, he had no sociological explanation for this. Moreover, under scrutiny, his underlying understanding of questions of sexuality and allegedly gendered behaviour were biogenic and psychogenic.

THE BOYS IN THE GANG

If Sutherland was forced to attempt to grapple with criminology's sex question, and tried (unsuccessfully) to resort to 'gender' as the explanation, the legacy of his work on the masculinity of the criminal pattern was clear in the emergence of subcultural theories of crime in the 1950s. Instead of forging a general theory of delinquency, then attempting to reconcile it with the sex question, Sutherland's protégé Albert K. Cohen placed the maleness of criminalities at the centre of his enquiries. In this respect, Cohen's *Delinquent Boys* (1955) was the first such criminological text in the English language. The cultural context of his book was a postwar alarm about youth gangs engaging in what Cohen described as 'non-utilitarian' (stealing for 'kicks'), 'negativistic', 'malicious' and versatile forms of delinquency (Cohen, 1955: 25–9). Cohen's trenchant critic, Walter Miller, author of rival texts in 1958, saw the delinquent ethos as affixed to masculinity and epitomised in the Marlon Brando movie, *The Wild One* (Kvaraceus and Miller, 1959: 66–7).

Cohen supported the stated view of his mentor, Sutherland, that the causes of the male dominance of delinquency were sociogenic—residing in gender ascriptions (cultural definitions of masculinity and femininity)—rather than biogenic. He believed, however, that certain gaps in differential association's explanatory grasp could be filled by blending in a degree of psychogenic causes for male criminal behaviour (Cohen, 1955: 17).

For Cohen the sex difference in delinquency could be explained quite simply. The purpose of the male delinquent subculture was primarily to help working-class males to strike out against a middle-class, respectable society in whose terms they could never adequately perform (Cohen, 1955: 119). He dubbed the delinquent the 'rogue male' with problems of adjustment (Cohen, 1955: 140). The delinquent male's values mirror those of the non-delinquent—being obsessed with achievement, exploitation, aggressiveness, daring, active mastery and pursuit (Cohen, 1955: 139). These correspond with the masculine role. No matter how disreputable the acts of the delinquent may be, he chooses acts that are characteristically masculine. This brings Cohen to his basic explanation of sex differences in criminality.

> Whereas the most highly ego-involved region in the boy's 'life space'
> . . . is that of performance and achievement relative to other boys, the
> corresponding highly ego-involved region for the girl is that of her
> relationships with the opposite sex . . . [T]he female's station in society,
> the admiration, respect and property she commands depend . . . on the
> kinds of relationships she establishes with members of the opposite sex
> (Cohen, 1955: 140).

Hence he contends that while the delinquent subculture offers a 'tailor-made' solution to problems of the male role, it is at best irrelevant to the vindication of the girl's status as a girl, and at worst it positively threatens her in that status 'as a consequence of its strongly masculine symbolic function' (Cohen, 1955: 143).

Cohen marries this tautological role theory—that is to say, men commit crimes because crime is masculine and women do not because crime is masculine—to the following psychogenic explanation. Both boy and girl children have a feminine identification with 'mommy'. She symbolises goodness, law and order. According to Parsons:

> The boy unlike the girl comes under strong social pressure to establish
> his masculinity, his **difference from** female figures. Because his mother
> is the object of the feminine identification which he feels is the threat
> to his status as a male, he tends to react negativistically to those
> conduct norms which have been associated with mother and therefore
> have acquired feminine significance. Engaging in 'bad' behaviour
> acquires the function of denying his femininity and therefore asserting
> his masculinity (Cohen, 1955: 164).

Having set up this sociogenic/psychogenic liaison, Cohen then introduces class differences as co-respondent. He contends that the relative social autonomy and the need to work or find sources of income quickly place the working-class boy in a better situation than his middle-class counterpart as regards masculine role affirmation. Prolonged economic dependence and close supervision by parents in high school and college years delay the middle-class boy's access to performance in the masculine role as a breadwinner. Delinquency helps him affirm masculine role identification. The working-class boy, by contrast, is able to build up definitions of masculinity

which are positive and independent, not merely negations of femininity . . . a richer . . . conception of the meaning of masculinity than the mere antithesis of goodness . . . therefore [he is] not likely to resort to 'badness' as a device to prove to the world that he is really masculine (Cohen, 1955: 165).

Hence, Cohen reasserts that it is class-status conflicts that motivate working-class males to crime, and the fact that delinquency is so symbolically masculine becomes an added extra. Since the majority of the population, and of delinquents, were working-class, this was a significant qualification of the status of acculturated masculinity in the genesis of delinquency. If the real motif for most delinquents is class conflict, Cohen has emptied even gender, as distinct from sex, of analytical force, demoting it to a merely descriptive place.

Walter Miller took issue with Cohen on the class conflict motif for delinquency. He insisted that delinquent behaviour was integrated and continuous with non-delinquent, urban, working-class behaviour and not a manifestation of class-status adjustment problems. Unlike Cohen, he did not set out to specify and explain the maleness of 'the wild ones' (Leonard, 1982: 134). He believed, however, following a psychoanalytic model, that the feminine identification problem as a criminogenic factor was more, not less, relevant to working-class boys than to middle-class boys. The reason he offered for this conviction was the fact that between a quarter and half of working-class boys resided in female-headed households—apparently a situation particularly undermining of their masculinity (Kvaraceus and Miller, 1959: 95–6). This argument led almost inexorably to his subargument that the lack of a masculine role model resulted in undue masculinity anxiety that could become compulsive. Miller believed that, unconsciously, working-class male delinquents from female-headed families desired to be caught, punished and supervised under the paternal authority of the police, judges and state prisons (Kvaraceus and Miller, 1959: 68; Miller, 1958).

Of these two subcultural theorists, Cohen is the one concerned to compare the situations of males and females. He observes that female delinquency is rare and specialised, confined to sexual deviance. Eileen Leonard has pointed out that Cohen hugely overpredicts the incidence of sexual delinquency in girls, ignoring the fact that girls' delinquencies are basically similar to boys', but that the system of criminal justice and its agents select the sexual aspects of girls behaviour as the basis for action against them, and not boys (Leonard, 1982: 13–3). Unfortunately, Cohen seems convinced that the problems and options of girls are fully covered by noting the culturally defined importance of catching a man. This effectively seems to consign women and girls to a static position outside class-status conflicts, indeed outside the masculine public sphere dominated by competing performing males. While Cohen does not speak of females in class terms as he does of males, it is possible to infer a kind of class analysis in his account of female sexual delinquency which mirrors his class analysis of male delinquency. Through their use of sexuality—as 'sluts'—working-class girls may be offering a specialised but analogous snub of the female sexual-status groups to which they may aspire but will fail to reach.

Cohen is confident that failure as a girl in the task of collecting men and viable relationships will always leave any other achievements whether as a 'career girl', a successful business woman or a brilliant student 'adulterated'. All of the alternative 'achievements' he cites are broadly white collar/middle class. Again he seems not to notice possible problems of applicability of this argument to the majority of women—working-class women. He offers a revealing analogy to convey to his imagined readership the gravity such a failure in the female role could signify for a woman.

> She may be compared to the engineer who achieves some gratification from success as an amateur musician but who thinks of himself first and foremost as an engineer . . . and who is judged by the community at large mostly by his performance in the occupation at which he earns his living (Cohen, 1955: 142).

Cohen's resort to gender role theory, though more central to his project than to Sutherland's, finally appears as barren and as merely descriptive as that of his mentor. The truth that his 1955 vision offers is a world of males judging their own value in terms of competitive performance against other males, and females judging their own value in terms of the degree to which they are valued by males. Employment of the sex/gender distinction has resolved nothing for postwar criminology, precisely because of the congruence of gender-role assignment and sex identity. The relationship between sex and gender does not prove to be arbitrary as this sociological distinction would wish to suggest. The entire reading of female persons offered by Cohen, for instance, derives from 'the male gaze' at their significance in the most basic senses. The girl represented as living only for the quest for appropriate male partners, perhaps could be seen as a clear blend of attributes of sex and of gender—but the former would seem to be responsible for the latter. Cohen's explanation for low rates of female delinquency and their high rates of conformity cannot be seen as markedly superior to those of Lombroso simply for being sociogenic. Like Sutherland, Cohen's use of gender describes rather than provides a basis for explanation of the position of the sexes in crime and delinquency. Moreover by displacing focus from sex to gender, men to masculinity or 'the masculine pattern', the places of *men*—'the wild ones'—are unexamined, disavowed by postwar criminology.

HOISTED ON THEIR OWN SEX/GENDER DISTINCTION

Feminist critics of masculinist criminology also have been enthusiastic users of the sex/gender distinction, especially following the publication of Stoller's book on the subject in 1968 (Gatens, 1983). Use of the sex/gender distinction was becoming increasingly commonplace during the 1960s and 1970s in the social sciences, the liberal humanities, and among humanist intellectuals and political activists. As noted above, the objectives of this distinction were to remove any necessary link between biological sex and gender attributes, capacities and behaviours. Put differently, it rendered the relationship between the sexed body and the acculturated gender as arbitrary.

The almost wholesale adoption of the sex/gender distinction within social theory becomes intelligible only within the wider context of intellectual discourses, characterised by the radical dichotomising of body and mind, nature and culture. This context allowed no social, cultural and psychical significance for biological facts such as sex. Moreover, the disallowing of these significances was premised on a narrowly anatomical, physiological definition of the biological body. Feminists had a strong interest in taking both as narrow and as negative a reading of the body as possible. For historically, misogynist discourses had sought rationalisation for women's subordination in those 'facts' of female biology discrepant from the male—reproductive capacities. A desire to flee the charge of closeness to nature and a wish to reduce the claims of the biological mark the feminist texts and strategies of the 1970s—and understandably so. Sociogenic 'gender' provided, feminists believed, a way out of the biological trap.

A thoroughgoing concern with gender is clear in feminist criminology. Biogenic criminologists of the past are denounced by feminist criminologists for their incompetent elision of sex and gender—attributing to nature what the reader is assured are socially constructed attributes of masculinity and femininity—that is to say, gender. It is fair to say that this has been a major, if not the main, argumentative strategy of feminist criminologists engaged in critique of earlier criminologies. In this work, stress is placed on the utter fluidity of gender roles, and the lack of universality in its content from culture to culture (see Smart, 1976: 56–60; Carlen, 1985: 2–9).

With this feminist brief in which the problematic of 'gender' is the point of interrogation, the postwar criminologists discussed above receive varying ratings and readings. Leonard's view of Sutherland is relatively favourable compared to others she reviews. Differential association

> provides a framework that in general terms explains . . . the criminality and non-criminality of men and women. [I]t is particularly helpful in emphasising that criminal behaviour is learned not psychologically or biologically determined. It reminds us that women are not permitted the same associations as men and, even within the same groups are treated unequally. Thus their crime rate can be expected to vary from that of men (Leonard, 1982: 114).

Her assessment of Cohen and Miller is much more negative. While she appreciates that Cohen at least recognises that males and females live in fundamentally different cultures, and that unlike Miller, he recognised that the subcultures he studied were male, with distinct values, roles, socialisation, expectations and opportunities, Leonard is vexed

> that Cohen deals with women in such a stereotypical manner . . . even if the perfunctory nod has been given toward the impact of social structure . . . Cohen disregards the subjugation of women and the fact that even when they achieve what is commonly expected of them (marriage and a family) they are still regarded as inferior to the male half of society (Leonard, 1982: 133).

Her overall complaint about criminology is its 'gender blindness', its sexism ('men or women are often simply omitted from study without sufficient reason for the exclusion of one sex') and the attribution of behaviour differences to biological or psychological rather than to social factors (Leonard, 1982: 183).

Leonard, like other feminist criminologists, is most concerned that criminology has not and for the most part cannot explain women's criminalities in terms that are of a sophistication comparable to those constructed to explain men's criminalities, that is, in non-biogenic and non-psychogenic terms (Heidensohn, 1968, 1985; Smart, 1976; Campbell, 1981; Scutt, 1976; Klein, 1976). On the other hand, Brown has sharply criticised the extent to which feminist criminologists have uncritically assumed the explanatory prowess of the categories 'social' and 'society':

the term society functions as the magic bullet (phallocentric imagery permitting) to show up the mistakes of criminology, ancient and modern. With the invocation of this powerful word biology and psychology may be exiled, all determinisms vanquished in the name of social origins and social change (Brown, 1986: 363).

In a more general context, Gatens has criticised the naive feminist adoption of the sex/gender distinction, understood by socialisation theorists as a body/consciousness distinction. Not only has this led to utopian and over-rationalist political strategies, but to fuzzy, unhelpful theoretical work attempting to engender an apparent neutralisation of sexual difference and sexual politics—amounting in reality to the 'masculinisation' of women (Gatens, 1983: 156). She insists on the necessary relation between the male body and masculinity, the female body and femininity; and moreover that this claim is neither biologism nor essentialism. Rather,

> [m]asculinity and femininity as forms of sex appropriate behaviours are manifestations of an historically based, culturally shared phantasy about male and female biologies and as such, sex and gender are not arbitrarily connected . . . Hence to treat gender, the 'symptom' as the problem is to misrecognise its genesis . . . To speak of 'acquiring' a particular gender is to be mistaken about the significance of gender and its intimate relationship to biology-as-lived in a social and historical context . . . It is not masculinity *per se* that is valorized in our culture but the *masculine male* (Gatens, 1983: 154).

Hence, for Gatens the focus on 'gender' in feminist theory is disastrous: a diversion that consigns feminism to the liberal humanist strategy of resocialisation or re-education with the objective of a 'degendering' of society. Such a strategy removes from men, whether individually or collectively, any responsibility for women's oppression—masculinity becomes the problem. Men are disavowed in this kind of feminist theory as much as in disciplines of knowledge such as criminology.

It would be incorrect to suggest that feminists set out to achieve this theoretical and political disavowal. Rather, it is the unintended consequence of the feminist flight from dominant understandings of biology and their implications for women. To locate any significant difference as biologically determined has been feared as tantamount to endorsing the unchangeable enslavement of women. Biology in such dichotomised understandings is cast as fixed, immutable, static and utterly outside culture. Yet as feminist critics suggest, these are not the only understandings of corporeality available or possible (Haug, 1987; Grosz, 1987b).

In fact assumptions about biology and its meaning for men and women are political constructions *par excellence*, best exemplified in their address of the sexed body. Grosz argues that social, economic, psychical and moral relations are not merely experienced by subjects, as it were in the mind, 'but are, in order to be experienced integrally recorded or corporeally inscribed' (Grosz, 1987b: 14). She contends that feminism can construct congenial theories of the body that place the biological elements as well as the constructed, socially informed or culturally specified elements (the body's capacity to be 'moulded') on a continuum. Rather than pitting biology in opposition to the cultural, feminism could stress the continuities. For biology

> must itself be amenable to psychical and cultural transformation to processes of retracing or inscription . . . [H]uman bodies created culture, and in the process, transform themselves *corporeally* (as well as conceptually). Human biology must be *always already* cultural, in order for culture to have any effect on it. It is thus a threshold term between nature and culture, being both natural and cultural . . . In short, human subjects give meaning to their biologies, to their bodies and their existence. This understanding of the body as a *hinge* or *threshold* between nature and culture makes the limitations of a genetic or purely anatomical or physiological account of bodies explicit (Grosz, 1987b: 15–16).

For feminist critics of the sex/gender distinction, its effects on feminist enquiries into masculinist knowledge formations has been to reduce their acuteness. With regard to the social sciences generally, gender

> became a means of absolving *men* from responsibilities for patriarchal domination: now it was attributed to masculinity, which, so it is presumed, is a characteristic of many women as well. There is a peculiar disassociation of the social from the corporeal, of the masculine from men and the feminine from women. Women are included as objects of analysis, and masculinity is attributed a negative status, but somehow what remains unexamined is men's place in the culture as *men* . . . [W]hat men do remains the province not of 'men's studies'; not a focus on men's masculinity, but on men as members of other groups—classes, races, professions, subcultures and so on (Grosz, 1987a: 3).

In short, men as *men*, are disavowed. It is they who remain 'the dark continent' of western knowledge formations.

Feminist criminology has been as much a prisoner as perpetuator of the discipline's longer-term disavowal of the place of men. While criticising criminology for its sexism, conceptual sloppiness and inadequate explanations, feminist criminology has sought more attention for women, claiming quite explicitly that criminology has been the study of men and crime (see Smart, 1976: 178; Heidensohn, 1985: 196; Leonard, 1982: 181). This claim seems to involve the inference that because it has failed to adequately explain feminine criminalities then, by default, what it has done is adequately explained the criminality of men. Arguably the feminist inference here is faulty. There is all the difference in the world between, on the one hand, undertaking enquiry into crimes and criminalisation as the sexed phenomena that they manifestly are, and, on the other hand, enquiring into crime 'sex-blind' with no acknowledged theory of the variable of sex. The former self-conscious approach may perhaps produce the criminologies of women and men (if there were grounds for this to be desirable); the latter will produce the blinkered gibberish that mainstream criminology so often has been. While critics like Cousins and Greenwood rightly sketch the bankruptcy of this discipline, especially its pursuit of the monolithic entity 'criminality', the discussion above raises a further question: namely, who have been the subjects and objects of the generalist criminological gaze in the absence of the thoroughgoing specification of sex? Not women, obviously; but clearly and equally, not men. If for some projects and causes, the way forward is the deconstruction of the criminological enterprise—and the case for this position is undoubtedly persuasive —it might, nonetheless, be interesting, possibly even useful, to know what a criminology of the sex 'men' could look like. For a feminism concerned with male practices currently classified as crimes against women, it may even be crucial.

Instead of adding 'women' as a neglected topic, if feminists must continue working in criminology they would do well to avow the place of men, to 'reinsert the male body into the discourses from which it has been expunged' (Gross, 1986: 135). A corollary of this may be to reject the notion of 'crime' as a sexually neutral category, a *human* activity, avowing instead its sex specificity. This would thoroughly displace questions of 'why are women more conformist than men?' or 'why are women's crimes different from men's?' and make it possible to ask

> what is it about men, not as working class, not as migrant, not as underprivileged individual, but *as men* that induces them to commit crime? Here it is no longer women who are judged by the norms of masculinity and found to be 'the problem'. Now it is men and not humanity who are openly acknowledged as the objects and subjects of investigation (Grosz, 1987a: 6).

ADRIAN HOWE

3 Sweet dreams: deinstitutionalising young women

The officially stated objective of Winlaton (Victoria's Youth Training Centre for Young Women) is 'to minimise harm done by social conflict' (Winlaton, 1987: 2).

All society is being harmed by a serious overkill in the processing of females, and in the long run the society will be irreversibly harmed (Sarri, 1976: 79).

. . . [I]nstitutions are not inherently and essentially brutalising and destructive. Rather, it is the particular practices constituting them that makes them so. The fact that such practices are not necessarily confined to the institution . . . means the struggle for change in juvenile justice cannot be satisfactorily waged through seeking to trap, confine or dismantle the power of the state, but requires more diverse and imaginative responses (Hogg and Brown, 1985: 410).

Writing is always agonising for me, but writing this chapter was especially gruelling for a number of personal and political reasons. The problem was not merely that what I kept wanting to say about the socially injurious nature of the state's handling of young women I had said before in another context (see, for example Howe, 1987a): more debilitating still, I was constantly reminded of a cartoon which I affixed to my filing cabinet during the last few dreadful weeks of completing my doctoral dissertation. The caption read: 'Go back, it's all been done before.' For the challenge in the field of the legal and social control of young women is to say something new, or at least to resist being overwhelmed by the feeling that it has all been said before. Indeed, of all the repetitive discourses of criminology and the sociology of 'deviance' and social control, none have become more repetitive than those on young women in the juvenile justice system. Over the past two decades, a surfeit of studies has focused on the state's handling of young women in Britain, the United States and, to a lesser extent, in Australia. We now know, because it has been demonstrated over and over again, that young women are arrested far less frequently than boys, that when they do appear before juvenile justice courts, most are processed for 'status offences' such as 'being in moral danger', and that they are more likely than boys to be incarcerated for such 'offences'.

For all that, this chapter is yet another intervention in the field. And although it has been beset by inertia and an unwillingness to become enmeshed in repetitive juvenile justice discourses, it is driven by desire—a desire to reflect on the politics of the legal and social control of young women. This reflection has been prompted by policy changes taking place in the child welfare and juvenile justice jurisdictions in Victoria, Australia.

VICTORIA'S BELATED 'REVOLUTION'

Over the last two years, Community Services Victoria (CSV) has released a series of discussion papers in anticipation of major legislative changes which it claims will change the face of juvenile justice in that state. In accordance with the Cain Labor government's 'social justice' commitments, CSV has outlined a reform package which, broadly, involves two major social policy shifts. First, CSV plans to 'redevelop' protective and correctional services for young people in institutional facilities. More specifically, the aim is to reduce the number of young people in institutional care by deinstitutionalising them and reintegrating them into the community through the development of community-based services. In this way, CSV hopes to follow policies and programmes which, when they were introduced in the United States in the 1970s, were hailed as a 'revolution in juvenile justice' (Hellum, 1979). Indeed, the changes brought about by the so-called 'reintegrative revolution' with its 'four Ds' policy themes of diversion, deinstitutionalisation, decriminalisation and due process, were acclaimed as being 'every bit as revolutionary' as the establishment of the juvenile court at the turn of the twentieth century (Empey, 1978, 1980).

Second, CSV has determined, following the recommendation of the Child Welfare Practice and Legislation Review Committee (CWPLR, 1985) which has provided the foundation stone for the 'new' juvenile justice policy, that the whole framework of Victorian juvenile justice be changed from its traditional focus—the welfare or 'best interests' of the child—to a focus on justice and rights for offending, neglected and abused young people. Couched in the familiar rhetoric of legalism (Collison, 1980), the new (not so new) 'justice principles' are that young offenders are entitled to the same due process rights as adults; that deeds and not needs are to be the focus of state intervention; that this intervention be based on the principle of the least coercive option; that services for young offenders be separate from those for non-offenders, and that diversion from the formal justice system be prioritised. CSV predicts that this shift from a welfare to a justice model of juvenile justice—a shift which is 'consistent with interstate and international developments' (Community Services Victoria, October 1986: 5)—will lead to a major upheaval in the juvenile justice arena.

Thus the 'Revolution' has finally come to Victoria, courtesy of CSV. Better late—fifteen years or so—than never. Whether the new policies will be revolutionary in any meaningful sense, whether they will mark a radical departure from the welfarist philosophy and practice of the juvenile justice system, remains to be seen. Certainly, the American evidence, as we will see, is not encouraging. My concern, however, is not to evaluate CSV's new policies—policies which have already been subject to widespread criticism (for example YAC, 1986; Fitzroy Legal Service, 1986). Still less do I wish to become enmeshed in the repetitions of the welfare-versus-justice debate which has dominated and all but exhausted juvenile justice discourse. Nor do I want to rehearse the tired old 'gender issues' of juvenile justice policy. My intention is rather to reflect on the meaning of deinstitutionalisation for young women at risk of criminalisation and/or state 'protection' and, in the process, to map out the contours of a more progressive, gender-specific juvenile justice strategy.

My starting point is the Victorian government's new juvenile justice policy. I then move from the outmoded welfare-versus-justice debate to a consideration of the processes of theorisation which have taken us from penology to the social analysis of 'penality' (Garland and Young, 1983: 2). I will argue that in order to understand the socially injurious nature of the state's handling of neglected, abused and offending young women, we need to comprehend that the status 'young woman' is an already injured, and therefore penalised status. I make no excuse for focusing on young women: they were singled out by the Review Committee as a 'special needs' group (CWPLR, 1985, Vol.I: 8), but were subsequently marginalised in policy recommendations, just as they have been throughout the history of juvenile justice (Schlossman and Wallach, 1978).

JUVENILE JUSTICE POLICY SHIFTS IN VICTORIA

The search for the meaning of the new CSV policy initiatives can take place at several different levels. Most immediately, what will the proposed legislative changes mean for young women at risk of incarceration in Victoria? An informed guess is not much: there are too many Catch-22s in the so-called 'Redevelopment' strategy, as one might expect from the mealy-mouthed, attenuated, let's-say-nothing-at-all rhetoric of liberal legalism in which the recommendations are clothed. 'Redevelopment', it turns out, is a euphemism for deinstitutionalisation, which is now government policy in that state. Following the Victorian Labor Party's 1985 election platform, which included a commitment to review all children's institutions to ensure that 'only those who represent a risk to themselves or to the community' be placed in institutional care (Community Services Victoria, May 1986), the government's stated aim is to deinstitutionalise as many young people as possible—both offenders and non-offenders on care and protection applications. Yet while the reduction of centralised, institutionalised care is said to be a major goal to be applied 'equally' to services for offending and non-offending young people, and while the stated goal is to promote community-based alternatives, 'less extensive deinstitutionalisation' is already anticipated for those young offenders deemed to be in need of 'a well resourced institutional sector'. And as for the 'non-offender', or rather the 'status offender'—a young person who has engaged in non-criminal behaviour such as running away, being uncontrollable or being exposed to abuse and exploitation—CSV's aim is to *'almost* [my emphasis] completely replace the need for any form of central institutional care' for these young people (Community Services Victoria, 1987: 14–15). Furthermore, in CSV's view, secure care will still be necessary for an undisclosed but small number of wards. The reform package designed by the Statewide Services Redevelopment Team to redevelop institutional services for young people therefore certainly does involve 'more than a straightforward process of deinstitutionalisation'—to borrow a CSV euphemism (Community Services Victoria, 1987: 11).

As for young women, the focus of this chapter, they have been marginalised yet again and for the usual reason: their small numbers, relative to boys, in youth training centres. In giving low priority to young women because of their minority status, CSV has duplicated traditional mainstream youth policy which has been accurately depicted by Mica Nava as 'largely a response to the "delinquent connotations" of "youth"'. Inasmuch as the implication is that girls do not need the same kind of regulation as boys, 'it follows that nor are girls properly "youth"' (Nava, 1984: 10). Furthermore, inasmuch as a major aim of the new policy is to deinstitutionalise young people, it is significant that CSV anticipates that the number of young women sentenced to detention will rise as a result of legislative changes. For example, more stringent guidelines for guardianship applications are expected to lead to the redefinition as offenders of young women currently institutionalised on protection orders. Again, changes to the maximum age jurisdiction of the Children's Court from 17 to 18 years, and the extension of sentencing to under-15-year-olds are also expected to increase the number of young women in correctional programmes in Victoria. However, as the rate of incarcerating young women in this state is more than double that of other states—in 1983 there were 51 young women incarcerated in Victoria (18.4 per 100 000), compared to 30 in New South Wales (8.6) and only 2 (2.3) in South Australia—CSV plans to reduce the average Winlaton population from 70 to between 20 and 40, in order to equalise the Victorian and New South Wales rates (Community Services Victoria, October 1986: 65; Community Services Victoria, 1987: 19).

So far as status offenders are concerned, it is well established that girls are institutionalised for status offences far more frequently than boys (see Chesney-Lind, 1977; Sarri, 1983). In Victoria, 90 per cent of admissions to Winlaton are wards, about 80 per cent of whom are admitted on non-neglect, that is, status offence, protection applications (Hancock and Chesney-Lind, 1985: 240–1). Further, it is well established that most (90 per cent by Winlaton's count) of these girls have been sexually assaulted at home. While the government was initially considering deinstitutionalising all status offenders, it was finally decided that 'secure care' programmes were required for these young people. According to the new policy, these 'protection' cases are now to be designated as young people who are 'a serious risk to themselves and who therefore require "secure care"' (Community Services Victoria, 1987: 36). The categories of 'risk to self' are: engaging or being likely to engage in actions which constitute a risk to themselves; and being 'voluntarily' sexually exploited by a third person 'normally for financial gain' (Community Services Victoria, May 1986: 8–9).

Several points are salient here. First, the change in designation does not change the reality: young women at risk of incarceration on protection grounds will continue to be incarcerated. Indeed, CSV explicitly defines 'risk to self actions' as 'actions which, if committed by an adult, would not normally warrant state intervention' (Community Services Victoria, May 1986: 7). The status offence is thus reincarnated. Second, the category 'risk to self'—namely, being sexually exploited for financial gain—will impact more heavily on young women. They will continue to find themselves incarcerated for prostitution. Third, CSV, responding to concerns raised by community groups about the limitations of the 'Statewide Redevelopment' policy, concedes 'the particular importance for young women' of the issue of sexual assault. Moreover, in the final analysis, CSV has also conceded that its proposed community-based alternative for 'at risk' young people—other families—is an inappropriate response to the prevalence of intra-familial sexual assault. It is heartening to learn that CSV has come to the view that it is not necessary for all Youth Accommodation and Support Scheme households to take the form of traditional nuclear families (Community Services Victoria, 1987: 73–4). However, to date, proposals for viable alternative support networks have failed to materialise. Consequently, we can reasonably expect to find young women deemed to be 'at risk to themselves' in the 'secure care' facility which is planned for Winlaton (Community Services Victoria, 1987: 36).

More broadly, what will the planned shift from a welfare to a justice model of juvenile justice mean for young women in Victoria? It will be recalled that the 'new' justice framework is to replace the traditional welfarist rationale for state intervention which was based on the 'best interests of the child' and a treatment ethic which sought to predict the young person's needs. Significantly, these 'unsound' welfare assumptions are now said to promote unjust state intervention, particularly in the case of young women who are too frequently proceeded against on protection applications, resulting in 'the imposition of what is in effect an indeterminate sentence'. That is, they are 'frequently incarcerated on moral grounds', rather than being charged for an offence. The problem—or, at least, a 'significant contributing factor'—has been 'the lack of viable alternatives to incarceration for young women' (Community Services Victoria, October 1986: 4–6). Planners of new services for young women must therefore recognise their 'different vulnerabilities and service needs'. However, these 'vulnerabilities' are identified merely as the effects of amalgamating services for offending and non-offending young women detained for care and protection. This is 'undesirable' in CSV's view, because it stigmatises the non-offenders and 'distracts attention from the social, rather than criminal, grounds for their incarceration'. Justice principles require that institutional facilities for offending young women be separated from those for non-offenders (Community Services Victoria, October 1986: 50–1).

Leaving aside, at least for the moment, questions about the nature of the 'social grounds' for incarceration (which, one expects, is a euphemism for abuse and exploitation), we need to note here that the adoption of 'justice principles' appears to come down, in the case of young women, to the separation of offenders and non-offenders.

Indeed, the adoption of a 'social justice perspective' is said to require, amongst other things, 'separating the legitimate basis of intervention' in care and protection cases from the 'legitimate basis of response to offending young people' (Community Services Victoria, 1987: 5). But in the case of young women, 'economic constraints and the inability to pursue ideal solutions' led CSV to make some critical decisions about relative priorities. While the boys are to be separated into different age groups, it was finally decided that it was not possible, given the small number of sentenced girls, to develop separate facilities for different age groups. Thus, notwithstanding CSV's tokenistic recognition of girls' 'different vulnerabilities', they remain a low priority within the new 'justice' scheme (Community Services Victoria, October 1986: 60–2).

MASCULINIST AND FEMINIST CRITIQUES

What are we to make of all this? From a progressive perspective—from any perspective—not much. CSV's reform package does not appear to have a potential to dramatically change the dismal status quo in the juvenile justice jurisdiction in Victoria. For example, the new category of 'risk to self' does not appear to change anything, and avoids the crucial question of how the 'risk' was created in the first place. More broadly, CSV's policy recommendations are unexciting, myopic and about what could be expected from a regurgitation of an unreconstructed justice model of juvenile justice. Perhaps not surprisingly, CSV appears to have ignored recent critical analyses in which the justice approach to criminal and juvenile justice has been thoroughly deconstructed and thus exposed as a shaky political strategy for progressive policy makers. Most crucially, critical analysts have pointed out that the concept of justice has been politically mobilised and 'colonised by the New Right' (Clarke, 1985: 417–18). For example, calls for tougher sentences are made in the name of justice, and the proposal to introduce 'secure care' orders, as Collinson observes, is a right-wing manoeuvre to introduce security into what is seen to be a 'soft' welfare jurisdiction (Collison, 1980: 164–5). Thus, there is nothing inherently progressive about the current revival of justice principles in criminal and juvenile justice politics (Hogg and Brown, 1985: 398; Clarke, 1985: 413). Furthermore, the deinstitutionalisation policy implemented in the American juvenile justice field in the 1970s and 1980s has been subjected to widespread criticism, at both the empirical and theoretical levels.

Shifting to this level of analysis, we find that endless empirical studies have demonstrated that the untheorised deinstitutionalisation strategy has, for the most part, failed to divert young people out of the juvenile justice system. The most repeated criticism is that of 'net-widening'—the most infamous of the so-called 'unanticipated consequences' of decarceration policy for youth (Klein, 1979). Net-widening has been amply demonstrated in studies of American community-based programs for juveniles implemented over the last 15 years.[1] These studies show that with few exceptions, notably that of Massachusetts, the programmes actually expand the net of social control. On the one hand, young people are merely being diverted from public to private institutions which, in the United States, take the form of privately-run welfare, psychiatric, detoxification and correctional facilities (Lemert, 1981; Lerman, 1984). On the other hand, 'wider, stronger and different nets' are extended over a wider group of young people as some, who were previously labelled 'status offenders', are re-labelled 'delinquents' and others, who were previously left alone, get moved into 'young person in need' regimes (Austin and Krisberg, 1981).[2] Significantly, the American research has shown that young women are especially vulnerable to further processing by the new programmes. Indeed, numerous empirical studies have shown that the decrease in the number of admissions of girls to public institutions in the United States has been offset by an increase in the number admitted to private correctional facilities (Krisberg and Schwartz, 1983: 343; Lerman, 1984: 12; Hancock and Chesney-Lind, 1985: 247; Krisberg et al., 1986: 26–8). More broadly, research has shown that despite the progress made in the United States in striking down legislation which clearly discriminates against young women, 'there is still evidence of differential treatment of delinquents by gender' and of the over-controlling of girls by the juvenile justice system for minor offences (Figueira-McDonough, 1987: 419).

In view of the availability of these widely canvassed research findings, we could have hoped that Victorian policy makers might have heeded the warnings about the realities of deinstitutionalisation. In particular, it would have been useful for CSV to consider the evidence indicating that young women will remain over-controlled by the juvenile justice system, even when legislation makes it more difficult to incarcerate them on 'protection' grounds. We can only hope that CSV will not report that the rising rate of incarcerated young women was an 'unanticipated consequence' of the deinstitutionalisation programme implemented in Victoria.

Moving onto the theoretical level of analysis, we find that decarceration policies have generated as much criticism here as at the empirical level. What is most striking about recent theoretical analyses is the near-hegemony of Foucauldian critiques of decarceration policy and its net-widening consequence—the proliferation of community-based corrections (Matthews, 1987: 44–6). The result is the so-called 'dispersal of discipline thesis' (Bottoms, 1983: 173–4), associated with the work of Stanley Cohen (1979; 1983). Following Foucault's notion of 'indefinite discipline', Cohen developed the so-called 'dispersal of discipline thesis' to examine how penal institutions are being developed in a community context. Key features of this thesis are the blurring of the boundaries between the institution and the community, the widening and thinning of the social control mesh, and the 'penetration' of the state into the community. This last concept is said essentially to sum up Cohen's thesis: as Bottoms explains, 'the formal social control agencies of the state are seen as penetrating more deeply into the informal networks of society' (Bottoms, 1983: 173–4). Or in Cohen's own words: 'The blurring of social control implies the deeper penetration of social control into the social body' (Cohen, 1979: 356).

Penetration, indeed, is the operative word in this masculinist social control theorising. It also looms large in the related field of informal justice where, Rick Abel, for example, claims that informal institutions allow state control to escape the walls of the prison and permeate society by processes of 'penetration and integration that are dispersed and all-encompassing' (Abel, 1982a: 6). Similarly, Garland and Young's collection of studies of 'penality' and the formation of the 'disciplinary' society, frequently resorts to the 'penetration' mode (Garland and Young, 1983). According to Barry Smart, for example: 'The penal process, from investigation to judgement and to the exercise of penality, has been penetrated by the disciplines and its "tools"' (Smart, 1983: 72).

Feminists can only be bemused by these penetrating—more penile than penal—masculinist analyses. But what are we to make of the alarmist visions conjured up by all the 'social control talk' about the dispersal of discipline and state control (Cohen, 1983; 1985)? Women can only gasp with incredulity at the futuristic scenarios conjured up by masculinist Foucauldian discourse—'the spectre of expanded state control . . . the nightmare of the benevolent state gone haywire' (Austin and Krisberg, 1981: 183, 188) and the emergence of a 'carceral archipelago' which provides for 'an intensity of intervention at least as great as that in most maximum security prisons' (Cohen, 1979: 352). For women have always been controlled and disciplined, if not in the state-controlled ways anticipated by the Foucauldian social control theorists, at least within 'civil society'. As feminist sociologists have reminded us, the social control of women takes many forms: it may be internal or external, implicit or explicit, private or public, ideological or repressive. Indeed, the 'primary sources' of such control are 'outside, or even beyond, judicial influence'—they are located within 'seemingly innocuous social processes' (Smart and Smart, 1978: 1–2). We know all this, moreover, from our own experience, and we know not to overemphasise the significance of the state in the control of women. Alternatively, we know that the 'spectre' of expanding state control is not self-evidently regressive for women, as our experience in the family, a site of oppression and control for many women, has demonstrated that there is nothing inherently progressive about the defence of 'a sphere of private, individual relations, autonomous of regulation' (Hogg and Brown, 1985: 409).

To focus specifically on young women—the subject of this chapter —we know that they are policed in everyday life; that they are sanctioned in their families more than boys; that they are policed by boys (and other girls) outside their family and that they are policed by a male-centred language focusing on their sexuality—'you slag, you mole, you frigid bitch' (Lees, 1986). We know, too, that this is a fiercely heterosexual society and we know how this impacts on girls, but more than we ever wanted to know about how this impacts on boys. More specifically, we know that girls are policed into hetero-sexual coupling relationships and trained for subordination to par-ticular males (Cain, 1986). Finally, we know that girls and women are coerced by privacy to the point where we can meaningfully speak of them living their lives in a 'private prison' (Stang Dahl and Snare, 1978). The concept of the 'private prison', unlike that of 'penetra-tion', is an important one for understanding the restraints placed on girls' and women's lives all along the freedom-imprisonment spec-trum. More specifically, it helps us to understand that the current state-imposed deinstitutionalisation policy will have minimal impact on girls' lives because the status 'girl' is already a sanctioned, and therefore, penalised, status.

We know all this not merely because feminist sociologists have told us as much in their evocative ethnographies of working-class girls' cultures and their resistances to the imperatives of femininity (see, for example McRobbie and Nava, 1984; Lees, 1986): we know all this because we are young women, or we have been. Unlike the 'knowledges' and predictions of masculinist Foucauldian social control analysis, our knowledge is grounded in experience—experience which must be the starting point for any effective feminist intervention in the juvenile justice arena.

We need to note in passing that recent revisionist, malestream theorising about social control is withdrawing from its more alarm-ist, state-focused 'dispersal of discipline' notions and, in the process, providing more useful points of departure for a clarification of the complex nature of the interplay of legal and social controls. Not-withstanding the fact that the revisionists suffer from a 'sanction myopia' which has so far precluded them from extending their masculinist gaze much further than civil sanctions (Freiberg, 1987:

243) and which has prevented them from understanding that social control—like criminality—is profoundly gendered (Cain, 1986), they are beginning to produce more insightful analyses. For example, recent work exploring the internal differentiation of the penal realm (Garland and Young, 1983: 15) and the dispersal of non-disciplinary as well as disciplinary forms of punishment (Bottoms, 1983) has obvious relevance for feminists. Furthermore, it is important to note in passing that Foucault's work is open to less alarmist, less penile and more feminist readings. For example, his methodological precautions about studying power 'at its extremities' and dispensing with a juridico-political concept of power (Foucault, 1980: 96–102) and his ideas about the establishment of a 'carceral network', understood as an extension of surveillance and of 'the power of normalisation' through-out society, connect in self-evident ways to feminist sociologies of the social control of women (Foucault, 1977: 300–8).

RETHINKING HARM—THE SOCIAL INJURY STRATEGY

Rather than explore these ideas, I want now to address directly the question of feminist intervention in the juvenile justice arena. In Garland's and Young's view—a view with which I concur—the desire to transform the study of punishment should be 'characterised by a healthy appreciation of the need to discuss policy' and to 'intervene in the practical' (Garland and Young, 1983: 5). Accordingly, I want to suggest a new direction for juvenile justice policy. My strategy is not based on a claim to transcend the 'pre-constituted dichotomies' of 'welfarism' and 'legalism' of juvenile justice discourse (Collison, 1980). Its originality lies rather in its prioritising of young women. It seeks to highlight the injurious nature of the state's intervention in their lives and also the injurious nature of their lived experience as women.

Indeed, the strategy is premised on this distinctive aspect of women's experience—namely, our injuries. I mean the hidden injuries of all gender-ordered societies, the injuries associated with lower gender status, the once privatised injuries which we have begun to name over the last two decades: domestic violence is now criminal assault in the home; incest is now father-daughter rape; sexual harassment, at least in the workplace, is now sex discrimination. But while these injuries have become public issues, they are still trivialised and dis-missed in the wider culture and legal culture. I have argued elsewhere that the vocabulary of law still has difficulty framing, and thus re-cognising, our claims because we have missed out a crucial step in our argument: insisting that our private injuries become public issues has not been enough. To ensure that our distinctive mode of alienation as women is not lost in its translation into a legal claim, we need to demonstrate that the injuries we feel at a private, intimate level are socially created, indeed, are social injuries, before we demand that they become public issues (Howe, 1987b).

I have borrowed the concept of social injury from Edwin Sutherland who had a different agenda to mine. By broadening the definition of crime to include all legally defined social injury for which the state provided a penalty, even if it was only a penalty in civil law, Sutherland achieved the distinction of bringing white-collar crime within the scope of criminology (Sutherland, 1945). I have already traced the development of the concept within post-Sutherland criminology and within the more fertile intellectual fields of American critical legal theory and Australian alternative criminology elsewhere (Howe 1987a; 1987b). For example, within the latter discourses, I noted the development of the notion of 'aggregate social harm', defined as 'those injuries, diseases and material losses' which are a consequence of 'deliberate policy or intentional behaviour which is collective and foreseeable'—such as industrial accidents, pollution and the manufacture of unsafe cars (Prisoners Action Group, 1980: 45–6), and I argued that feminists could profitably intervene in the process of redefining foreseeable social injuries and developing a new common-sense understanding of socially injurious behaviours. In this connection, I noted that American feminist legal theorists have begun the crucially important work of theorising women's gender-specific injuries, such as sexual harassment, as group-based social injuries (MacKinnon, 1979; West, 1987; Howe, 1987b).

Interestingly, too, the concept of 'harm' has recently re-emerged in the field of victimology. According to Freiberg, harm is an 'underdeveloped concept, but one of crucial importance' in the determination of appropriate sanctions within victimology (Freiberg, 1988: 23–4).

In relation to our present concern, all of these discursive developments aid in the elaboration of what might be called a social injury strategy for empowering young women, especially those young women at risk of state intervention in their already sanctioned lives. This strategy is empowering because it provides them with a language for naming their more injurious life experiences, such as sexual abuse, exploitation and discriminatory treatment in their homes, in schools, in the workplace and in the juvenile justice and welfare systems. If they can name these injuries, young women can begin to develop a sense of injury and a sense of entitlement to redress. Oppressed, victimised, outsider groups—such as young women within the juvenile justice system—need to know that they have entitlements. The social injury strategy provides them with a sense of entitlement because it addresses the problem of the privatised nature of their pain by creating a language with which they can communicate that pain and make it public knowledge (Stang Dahl and Snare, 1978). The strategy enables them to speak out about how their injuries have hurt them. Moreover, it provides them with a vocabulary which they can understand because they already use it. Hear these 17-year-old survivors of intra-family rape: 'There's a lot of hurt left inside me . . . I've got so much hurt . . . '; ' . . . I got a scar, a mental scar and I've tried to shake it off and it's not working' (Women's Coordination Unit (NSW), 1986: 87–8).

More broadly, the social injury strategy provides young women at risk of state intervention with agency—that is, with an ability to exert influence and power not mediated through either adult authority (Hogg and Brown, 1985: 405) or male adolescents. By helping to politicise their gender-specific injuries, the concept of social injury gives these young women standing to speak. By helping them to develop a new common sense about social injuries, it gets at the problem of exposing covert forms of oppression and control by revealing that these are located in the social sphere and not in their own minds or personal lives.

The social injury strategy has other advantages. First, it crosses discursive boundaries in order to find young women's injuries a place in the broader theoretical movement which is developing the concept of injury in ways which are intended to transform common-sense understandings of relative social harms and to impact progressively on law. For example, it involves feminist policy makers and young women themselves in the process of redefining foreseeable social injuries, a process started by Australian alternative criminologists in the early 1980s. Second, the strategy enables us to add young women's injuries to the list of substantive areas which critical legal scholars have suggested need to be examined in order to transform 'unperceived injurious experience (unPIE)' into 'perceived injurious experience (PIE)' (Felstiner, Abel and Sarat, 1981: 634). While naming is already a feminist strategy, construing women's social injuries as 'PIEs' may help to legitimate women's entitlement to a remedy. In particular, it may help male-dominated courts to see women's injuries as 'harm of a kind in which the state has legitimate interest' (MacKinnon, 1985b: 61). More broadly, the social injury strategy finds legitimation—for those who need it—outside feminist discourse.

It is significant, in this respect, that the concept of 'harm' has now entered the discourse of child welfare and status offender jurisdictions. This reflects the view that state intervention should be premised on specific harms to a child, rather than on the basis of parental conduct. Elaborating on this view, one British study recommended that only the following categories of harm be admitted: where the child is 'likely to suffer a serious injury'—a physical, emotional or sexual injury—and where the intervention would not create 'a greater harm' (Taylor et al., 1979, 87-8). Importantly, 'harm' is the key concept in the 'new' philosophy of 'children in need of care' which is being introduced in Australian status offence legislation. New South Wales, the Northern Territory, the Australian Law Reform Commission and now the Victorian government have proposed abandoning the old 'exposed', 'uncontrollable' and 'truant' categories of status offender in favour of 'the child in need of care'. The aim of the new formulation is to prevent harm to the child. For example, one of the reasons for which a child might be in need of care is that 'he [sic] is being, or is likely to be, harmed as a consequence of his [sic] behaviour or the conduct of persons with whom he [sic] is residing ...' This is the New South Wales formulation for limiting intervention—the family is not to be disrupted unless the conduct is likely to cause the child harm (Gamble, 1985: 103).

In Victoria, the draft Children's Bill designed by Terry Carney's Review Committee defined a child in need of protection as one who 'has suffered a substantial harm through physical injury, sexual abuse or psychological damage' (CWPLR, 1985, Vol. III). This formula was altered to 'significant harm' in the Children and Young Persons Bill which was introduced in November 1987. (However, the Bill was not passed until 14 June 1989, and it had not commenced operation by the end of 1989.) A child in need of protection now includes the following categories: one who has suffered, or is likely to suffer 'significant harm' resulting from physical injury or sexual abuse; one who has suffered or is likely to suffer 'emotional or psychological harm of such a kind that his/her development is likely to be significantly damaged'; or one whose physical development or health has been or is likely to be 'significantly harmed' and the child's parents have not protected, or are unlikely to protect, the child from 'harm of that type'. Thus, the notion of harm—'significant harm'—has become the key component in the Victorian definition of a child in need of protection.

As Helen Gamble observes, the new 'harm' justification for intervention may well have been implicit in the old status offender definitions, but in practice 'management problems' were prioritised over the issue of harm to the child. Now at least, the question of harm is explicit. However, Gamble is concerned that the concept is vague and open to abuse and that, in particular, the concept of 'likely to be harmful' is discretionary and 'subjective'. In her view, it is possible that 'early sexual experiences may be interpreted as behaviour likely to cause harm to the child', which could lead to 'premature intervention' (Gamble, 1985: 105-6).

It is precisely statements such as these which underline the usefulness of the social injury strategy and the need for feminist intervention in the definitional process. Just what, exactly, does Gamble mean by 'early sexual experiences'? If we take one of the most prevalent forms, namely father-daughter rape, my strategy requires that we recognise it as a massive social harm and that we challenge masculinist interpretations and trivialisations of that harm.[3] It is important, too, that we deconstruct the euphemistic language of social control talk and expose the vague 'social grounds' for the incarceration of girls (Community Services Victoria, October 1986: 50–1) for what they too frequently are—conditions of abuse, exploitation and discrimination. The introduction of the concept of 'harm' provides some ground for optimism in this area, but we need to be careful. For example, the categories of children in need of care contained in the new Northern Territory's child welfare legislation—namely, engaging in conduct which constitutes a serious danger to his [sic] health and safety, or is harmful or potentially harmful to the general welfare of the community (Gamble, 1985: 105)—fall short of the standards of the social injury approach which I am suggesting here. Determining whether a young person has engaged in 'harmful' conduct must not be reduced to a question of determining whether he or she has done something harmful. A feminist social injury strategy would ensure that any assessment of the seriousness of the harm—that is, of the social injury involved—must include an assessment of the harms done *to* young people, particularly to young women, whether these occur in the home in the form of male sexual abuse, in the courts in the form of discriminatory sentencing, or in institutions where they have been, and will continue to be, incarcerated, for their 'protection'.

At the same time, a feminist assessment of the seriousness of threats to the health, safety and welfare of young women and of the community would need to consider possible harms inflicted by deinstitutionalisation policies. For while the decriminalisation of status offenders is supposed to liberate young people, especially young women, from an outmoded 'exposed-to-moral-danger' morality, and while it may reduce police harassment of working-class girls, 'it might also do lasting harm to them' (Empey, 1980: 171). After all, 'the community'—the new designation of this target population—is a 'space of regulation' (Burchell, 1981: 89–92). It is also frequently a place of unemployment, homelessness, exploitation, violence and 'benign neglect' (Hogg and Brown, 1985: 402). Feminists need to assess all these factors in their determination of serious harms or social injuries.

Finally, my social injury strategy satisfies the requirement laid down by juvenile justice analysts for a progressive juvenile justice strategy today. For example, it satisfies the requirement that we move beyond the outmoded welfare-versus-justice models of juvenile justice, that we avoid being trapped in a constant recycling of 'justice' versus 'welfare' principles, and that we politicise legal and welfare agencies involved in juvenile justice (Clarke, 1985: 421). A feminist strategy is by definition a politicised strategy, and mine is more than a simple deconstruction of 'justice' or a restatement of the 'virtues' of welfarism. While acknowledging that the welfare framework at least highlights the 'social character' of the individual—in particular, the overrepresentation of working-class young people in the juvenile justice system (Clarke, 1985: 415–18)—my social injury strategy reconceptualises the whole 'youth' problem by providing a more progressive contextualisation of the lives of young women at risk of state intervention. On the one hand, the strategy requires that young women's gender specific injuries—for example, sexual harassment— be reconceptualised as legally cognisable injuries. On the other hand, the strategy provides an understanding of the socially injurious context of young women's acts of survival. It thus moves beyond the welfare-justice conundrum but without sinking into an ineffectual and idealist 'politics of transcendence' which naively attempts to transcend the pre-constituted dichotomy of the penal–versus–assistantial which forms the public common–sense understanding of juvenile crime and child welfare (Collison, 1980).

Closer to home, the social injury strategy satisfies several of the requirements laid down by Hogg and Brown for a progressive Australian juvenile justice policy. In particular, it does not assume that the juvenile justice system is a discrete homogenous system which can be transformed in isolation from wider social relations and it does not assume that community-corrections programmes are progressive or liberating. On the other hand, it does try to provide a social analysis of juvenile justice and a consideration of the conditions of possibility of social change (Hogg and Brown, 1985: 399–400). The social analysis is that of the socially harmful nature of the injuries suffered by young women; the possibility of social change which the social injury strategy suggests is centred on the concept of injury. For injury's strength is not only that it is readily understood by young people: it is also legally cognisable—it has actionable status. Unlike 'oppression', many forms of injury have become actionable, as the history of tort and contract law and the evolution of workers' compensation demonstrates (Abel, 1982b; Friedman and Ladinsky, 1967). We may not like the way injury is currently constituted by law, but we can at least recognise its potential to be reinterpreted in progressive ways. Finally the social injury strategy is designed, as I have already argued, to empower young people—specifically, young women—by restoring agency to them (Hogg and Brown, 1985: 405).

I can already hear the chorus of objections. First, it will be said that encouraging young women to speak up about their injuries perpetuates a victim mentality and a victimised I-hurt-therefore-I-am-injured self-identity. Certainly, we do not need a strategy in which women are constituted as victims. However, the social injury strategy would enable young women to see themselves as survivors, not victims. Most crucially, it would provide them with a vocabulary of resistance in which to express personal, experiential knowledge, including knowledge of their mothers' and their older sisters' lives— knowledge which contradicts and challenges normative evaluations of marriage and motherhood (Lees, 1986).

Second, we need to consider the vexed question of 'subjectivity'. In an updated version of Paul Tappan's concern that the concept of social injury did not define what is injurious, but 'merely invites the subjective judgements of the investigator' (Tappan, 1947), David Trubek has expressed reservations about the 'complex subjective dimension' of the notion of an 'unperceived injurious experience' (Trubek, 1981). Similarly, Gamble finds the concept of conduct which is 'likely to be harmful' subjective (Gamble, 1985: 106). Yet the advantage of this concept is that at least it makes explicit the notion of harm or injury. It was implicit in the old status offence definitions: girls were seen to be harmed by their own sexuality, rather than by rapist family 'friends'. It is not, then, that we do not already have a conception of conduct 'likely to be harmful': the problem is rather that of masculinist hegemony in the definitional process. Explicit references to 'harm' or 'likely harm' in child welfare legislation opens up the question of harm or injury to young women who could profitably intervene in the struggle over definitions of serious harm.

Finally, it will no doubt be objected that my social injury strategy is discriminatory because it privileges young women. It may be objected too, that this provides the foundation for a bifurcated juvenile justice system of hard (boys) and soft (girls) options which will discriminate against boys. Yet, significantly, young women are being recognised as a special needs group in recent Australian child welfare and juvenile justice jurisdictions. For example, in Victoria, Carney's Review Committee singled out as special needs groups 'children from Aboriginal families, ethnic communities, disabled children, adolescents and, *in particular*, adolescent girls' [my emphasis]. Furthermore, the committee, in recognising the 'special needs' of adolescent girls in particular, claimed that its proposals were aimed at 'shifting emphasis away from individual problems to recognition of the social and economic forces which discriminate against young people' (CWPLR, 1985: 8). Again, the Women's Coordination Unit in New South Wales, recognising that girls in care and girls at risk have 'special needs', has proposed that affirmative action principles be incorporated into the delivery of all services to girls. Indeed, the unit has specifically recommended that the Legal Aid Commission recognise young women as a 'special needs category' (Women's Coordination Unit, 1986: 9–16). In the final analysis, however, my answer to the objection that I am favouring girls is quite simple: history and endless empirical studies have demonstrated that juvenile justice systems have always discriminated against girls and treated them as marginal to a system designed for boys (Schlossman and Wallach, 1978; Huntington, 1982). Isn't it time for a change?

REGINA GRAYCAR

4 Equality begins at home

Australia, like many other western capitalist countries, has responded
to the resurgence of the women's movement over the past two decades
by enacting legislation at the federal level and in some states designed to secure formal legal equality between women and men.
Anti-discrimination laws in New South Wales, Victoria, South
Australia, Western Australia and the Commonwealth proscribe discrimination on the grounds of sex, marital status and pregnancy in
areas of 'public' life concerning the workplace and the market, such
as employment, education, accommodation and the provision of goods
and services. In some jurisdictions, further steps have been taken to
provide for equal employment opportunity for women and some
minority groups through affirmative action programmes (see Ronalds,
1987).

My concerns in this chapter are twofold. First, equality measures
of this kind, essential as they are, have the potential to paper over,
and perhaps to entrench, the persisting material inequalities between
women and men in other areas of social life not so readily identified
as the 'public sphere'. I refer in particular to the regulation of family
relations and state income support policies, particularly those addressed at single parent (overwhelmingly women-headed) families.
Secondly, the 'ideology of equality' has been appropriated from its
place in the quest for the advancement of women's interests by deeply
conservative groups such as fathers' rights activists and opponents of
equal employment opportunity for women, and has been harnessed
as a weapon in the battle for the maintenance of male dominance.
I conclude in this chapter that women's social and economic positions have not been significantly advanced by the measures described
above and that the progression toward that advance, such as it is, is
in danger of being thwarted by a backlash of considerable force.

These propositions are illustrated with particular reference to 1980s debates about child custody, though they are also supported by developments in other areas of family law and policy such as child maintenance, matrimonial property and federal income support practices, each of which will be briefly touched upon in this chapter.

CHILD CUSTODY AND DISCOURSES OF EQUALITY

Historically, fathers had absolute rights to the guardianship of their legitimate infant children, even to the extent that, on their death, they could will away guardianship of the child, irrespective of the mother's wishes (see Barblett, 1980; Dickey, 1985; Finlay, 1983; Radi, 1979). Once the equity courts were given power to consider applications for custody from mothers, according to principles under which the welfare of the child came to be considered as paramount, the courts began to elevate the status of motherhood into a sacred, biologically essentialist virtue. This led to the development of the 'tender years' doctrine, under which young children, particularly girls, were considered to be best looked after by their mothers in the event of separation or divorce. As one judge in New South Wales put it in 1976:

> I am directed by authority to apply the common knowledge possessed by all citizens of the ordinary human nature of mothers . . . That knowledge includes an understanding of the strong natural bond which exists between mother and child. It includes an awareness that young children are best off with both parents, but if the parents have separated, they are better off with their mother. The bond between a child and a good mother . . . expresses itself in an unrelenting and self-sacrificing fondness which is greatly to the child's advantage. Fathers and stepmothers may seek to emulate it and on occasions do so with tolerable success. But the mother's attachment is biologically determined by deep genetic forces which can never apply to them (*Epperson v Dampney*, 1976 per Glass JA at 241).

As we know from our recent history, feminists came to challenge the notion that women were innately suited to motherhood, since it followed, in some of the renditions of this view, that they were suited to little else. This biologistic account also presumes that men are neither capable of being, nor willing to be, primary caregivers. Their fatherhood role, so the conventional wisdom went, was best served by removing themselves from the home for many hours a day to earn the money to support their women and children. Men are the bread-winners; women the dependants and child carers. It was this con-struction of domestic life that came under challenge from feminism. Feminists wanted men to take more responsibility for the care of their children and to spend more time with them—and not just leisure time, but feeding and bathing etc. The recognition that an increasing number of women work outside the home—even if much of that work is part-time, badly paid 'women's work'—led to campaigns about the provision of childcare, still grossly inadequate in Australia. It followed that feminism required the rejection of biologist notions of mothers' innate capacity and suitability for the care of children.

In 1976, Australian family law underwent something of a revolution when the Family Law Act 1975 (Cth) came into force. The Act, which since 1988 deals with custody of *all* children, including ex-nuptial children, provides that in the absence of a contrary order, both parents are guardians of any child and have joint custody (s.63F).[1] Guardianship refers to the legal responsibility, sometimes called 'legal custody' in other jurisdictions, while 'custody' (prior to 1983, 'care and control') refers to what is often called elsewhere 'physical custody'. In disputed cases of guardianship, custody or access, the Family Court is directed to regard the 'welfare of the child as the paramount consideration' (Family Law Act 1975 (Cth), s.60D). In 1979, the High Court of Australia expressly rejected the 'tender years' doctrine, or the mother principle, stating in *Gronow v Gronow* that this had never been a rule of law, but was rather a 'canon of common sense founded on human experience'. The court said that '[i]n earlier days, when there was no role for a father in the upbringing of children and in the running of a household', these matters were left entirely to mothers. But the court went on to state, without citing any evidence for this, that

> there has come a radical change in the division of responsibilities
> between parents and in the ability of the mother to devote the whole
> of her time and attention to the household and to the family. As
> frequently as not, the mother works, thereby reducing the time which
> she can devote to her children. A corresponding development has been
> that the father gives more of his time to the household and to the
> family (*Gronow v Gronow*, 1979 per Mason and Wilson JJ at 528).

This rosy picture of domestic life, where housework and childcare are shared, does not accord with any of the empirical evidence in Australia which tells us that women who work outside the home are still primarily responsible for the domestic work (see Game and Pringle, 1984; Bryson, 1985; Russell, 1983). But courts and judges sometimes seem to prefer assertion, rather than hard data, when discussing the practices of domestic life (for an interesting discussion of this phenomenon, see Davis, 1987). These assumptions about 'recent changes in the practices of domestic life' are as widespread as they are ill-founded. One New South Wales judge, speaking at a seminar on accident compensation, in the context of a discussion about compensating women for their loss of capacity to do domestic work after an injury (see Graycar 1985a; 1985b), asserted:

> Those incidentally who care to dabble in jurimetrics might care to consider what is to be made of this: of the seven wives of the seven judges of the Court of Appeal, three are in full-time professions, and occupations, two are in part-time professions or occupations, one was in full-time employment before marriage, and the remaining one in part-time employment before marriage. I would think therefore that all of us have experience of what might be regarded as a more modern way of life, in which household tasks are shared (Samuels, 1982: 311).

It follows on from this conventional wisdom that, since mothers and fathers (at least where mothers work outside the home) share responsibility for the running of the household and the children, there is accordingly no basis for preferring either of them as a custodial parent. This is reflected to some degree in the case law where a number of fathers have been awarded custody after a dispute with a mother who works outside the home. In some of those cases (for example *Harrington v Hynes*, 1982; *Mathieson*, 1977) the courts have characterised the parents as labouring under 'equal handicaps' as potential custodians in being full-time workers: this despite the fact that in both of these examples, the father had made it clear that the children's day-to-day care was to be delegated to other women —in one case, a new wife, and in the other, the father's mother, sister and eldest daughter.

One particularly egregious example of this relatively recent phenomenon received some public notoriety in 1987 when questions were raised about the case in the Senate. There, two professional parents (both are medical practitioners) went to the Family Court in Adelaide in a dispute over custody of their children (*W v W*, 1987). The judge initially awarded the wife custody on a conditional basis: on 6 August she agreed to the wife having custody *if, but only if,* she resigned her job and was pregnant by 7 October. In her judgment on 6 August, Murray J had stated: 'The major question mark hanging over the wife . . . is whether she would be prepared to sacrifice her career for the sake of the children.' The wife had told the court that she wished to complete her examinations and continue to work part time. She had also given evidence that she planned to have another child with her new husband. The judge decided that the wife would not give up her job—'she wants her cake and eat it too [sic]— unremarkable in these days of equality of opportunity' (*W v W*, 1987 at 19). When they came back to the court on 7 October , and the wife had not become pregnant, she awarded custody to the father, despite the fact that she had earlier commented that the father, at 57, was more like a grandfather to them. There was, of course, no suggestion that he give up his job in order to qualify as a suitable full-time parent, and it was made clear in the judgment that his new wife would undertake the day-to-day care of the children, both of whom were school-aged girls (11). An expedited appeal against this decision was allowed by the Full Family Court in December, 1987 and the matter was settled prior to a retrial (*Swaney v Ward* (1988)).

Overseas, feminist commentators have noted a recent tendency for courts to award custody to fathers and for legislatures to provide for statutory joint custody as a starting point in disputed cases (see, for example Schulman and Pitt, 1982; Boyd, 1989). It is easy to see how joint custody can be perceived as the quintessential manifestation of 'equality' in the area of child custody. After all, haven't women complained that men have not taken sufficient responsibility for their children? However, as a number of American commentators have pointed out, 'joint custody' has a range of disparate meanings covering a variety of situations, with the result that there is no guarantee that a court order of joint legal custody has any real effect on the day-to-day caretaking practices of parents. In the United States, the overwhelming majority of statutory joint custody regimes deal only with the legal rights and responsibilities, leading a number of commentators to point out that joint custody looks more like sole maternal custody (in the sense of care and control) with access or visitation by the father (see, for example Schulman and Pitt, 1982; Fineman, 1988).

It is not only working mothers who have lost custody cases for failure to conform to idealised notions of motherhood: lesbian mothers, whether working or not, have also caused concern to Family Court judges (see, for example Anon, 1980).

A totally different approach is documented by Phyllis Chesler in her *Mothers on Trial: The Battle for Children and Custody* (1986). She notes a disturbing trend of awarding custody to fathers on the basis that the mothers were only 'stay-at-home' mothers and therefore the child would have better educational opportunities and material advantages and receive more stimulation by living with the father. A variant, in the case where both parents work outside the home, is to award custody to the father because of his superior economic position. To favour the more economically advantaged parent is a paradigm example of applying a supposedly gender-neutral rule in a highly gender-specific context. Given the extraordinary wage gap between women and men in Australia, which flows from a highly gender-segmented workforce (see Ronalds, 1987; Women's Bureau, 1988), it is clear that were such a rule to be adopted in Australia, women would lose custody of their children almost as a matter of routine. Men both earn more money than women and repartner much more frequently than women, thereby enabling them to offer the children a stable 'nuclear' family environment.

Catharine MacKinnon has commented on this trend:

> In effect, [men] get preferred because society advantages them before they get into court, and law is prohibited from taking that preference into account because that would mean taking gender into account . . . So the fact that women will live their lives, as individuals, as members of the group women, with women's chances in a sex-discriminatory society, may not count, or else it is sex discrimination (MacKinnon, 1987: 35).

So far there is little evidence of either of these phenomena in the reported Family Court cases—but it must be noted that few cases are actually reported. However, there has recently been considerable agitation for the establishment of a joint custody norm to be applied by the Family Court in Australia. Interestingly, despite the fact that initially it was feminists who wanted men to share the care of children, most of the recent support for joint custody has come from men. Some of it derives from reputable sources such as the Institute of Family Studies (see Edgar, 1986) and the Family Law Council (1987), which in its report on access, also recommended a move toward joint custody (without, however, explaining precisely what is contemplated by this proposal).

Former legal academic Geoffrey Lehmann conducted a vigorous campaign in the early 1980s for the establishment of a joint custody norm. He and other fathers' rights advocates argue that fathers are discriminated against when it comes to child custody. In one of Lehmann's publications on the subject (Lehmann, 1983), he stated:

> If men can have their children confiscated from them irrespective of their own moral worth and effort, then they will be obliged to avoid marriage, vasectomize themselves, become narcissistic and use women as sexual objects (p. 62) . . .

> Sole custody is an anachronistic survival from fault divorce and an era when there was, in effect, a legal presumption against men to balance the discrimination against women elsewhere in society.
> Joint custody would appear to benefit children and parents. It is a script for equality. We are proud of our anti-discrimination laws, yet continue to discriminate against non-custodial mothers and fathers. We harass the latter for maintenance payments for children but deny them a normal parental relationship (p. 66).

A significant base for the joint custody campaign is the growing number of fathers' rights groups which have increased not only in number but also in political clout, to the extent that one of their most vocal spokespersons was a member of the influential Child Support Consultative Group. In 1986, the Australian Law Reform Commission, which was undertaking an inquiry into the law of contempt, held a series of public hearings around Australia. The majority of those who gave evidence did so in response to the Contempt and Family Law part of the inquiry (though this constituted only one aspect of the reference which also covered civil and criminal contempt generally). Forty-six of the 71 oral submissions were from fathers' rights groups such as the Lone Fathers' Association, Men's Confraternity, Families Against Unnecessary Legal Trauma (in Divorce) (FAULT), Family Law Action Group, Parents Without Rights, Family Law Reform Association, Divorce Law Reform Association, or from individuals sympathetic to their position. These organisations also made seven written submissions (see Australian Law Reform Commission, 1987a: 605–9). Although the specific focus of the hearings was on the use of contempt powers in the Family Court, particularly with regard to access problems, a number of other themes emerged.

First, these men believe themselves to be the victims of discrimination by the Family Court, which is run, in their view, by 'radical feminists'. It should be noted here that earlier, similar claims by the 'Army of Men' were taken up by the Family Court's research section in 1983 (see Horwill and Bordow, 1983: 1) and led to the publication of a report demonstrating that when men actually contested custody, over 40 per cent of cases were resolved in their favour (Horwill and Bordow, 1983). Yet to read the transcripts, one would think that men were never awarded either sole or joint custody of their children.

To counter this 'discrimination', they submitted that the courts should be bound to award joint custody which they argued was 'working fantastic' in California. (Interestingly, California has recognised the disadvantages of joint custody for women and children and in 1988 repealed the law providing preference for joint custody dispositions: see *San Francisco Chronicle*, 2 September 1988: A14.)

Another common theme that emerged was their avowal to refuse to pay maintenance if they do not get access to their children. This 'no access-no maintenance' refrain is a matter of great concern in the context of the national Child Support Scheme, established in 1988, which involves requiring non-custodial parents to pay a set proportion of their incomes in child support, in some cases by means of automatic withholding from wages.[2] In a statement to Parliament in March 1987, announcing the establishment of the Child Support Scheme, federal Social Security Minister Brian Howe stated that access and maintenance would not be linked as part of the new scheme (Howe, 1987: 1370). The men's groups obviously do not accept this and have continued to state publicly that they will not co-operate unless they get more access to their children.

The final, disturbing common theme that emerges from the men's evidence is the frequent reference to, and evident sympathy for, the terrorist violence which has been directed at the Family Court and which is also becoming more prevalent outside that Court. One commentator, in a 1985 annual survey of family law in Australia, stated:

> Instead of terrorist attacks on judges of the Family Court of Australia and on legal practitioners, dissatisfied parties—invariably, thus far, fathers involved in custody disputes—have responded by killing the children in dispute and themselves (Bates, 1986: 17).

Judith Allen has suggested, though she stresses that her information is anecdotal, that access and custody demands by fathers have been more willingly granted by the court in light of the recent violence, even where they might otherwise have been perceived as not in the best interests of the child (Allen, 1985: 132).

It is essential that we do not underestimate the influence of these fathers' rights groups and, even more importantly, that we listen to the language they use, replete as it is with references to 'equality' and 'discrimination'. In 1986, a series of newspaper and television advertisements appeared calling for 'Victim fathers to fight for rights' (see *Sydney Morning Herald* 6 November 1986), and stating that 'sometimes the best mothers are fathers'. And, in October 1987, a *Sydney Morning Herald* columnist published a manifesto of the Perth-based Men's Confraternity. It was their spokesperson, Mike Ward, who told the Law Reform Commission in 1986 that 'the Family Court . . . is organised by radical feminists . . . So when a man goes in . . . he is guilty until proven otherwise' (Australian Law Reform Commission, 1986: 378).

He also suggested:

> Misogynist is, you know, a hater of women if you like. There is no such word in the English language for a hater of men. We call it Ryanism[3] for obvious reasons (Australian Law Reform Commission, 1986: 380).

The group's manifesto (see *Sydney Morning Herald* 16 November 1987) states that Men's Confraternity was established in response to concern

> about discrimination against men in pensions, law, welfare and education. Concerned about continual attacks on men, led by men-hating feminists, who have entrenched themselves in positions of power and influence, in government, media and education.

Their aim is not to obtain equality but total domination of men at all levels . . . We are concerned also at the continual attacks by feminists at the family unit, which have created a society of single-parent families, made motherhood a dirty word, and also to put the job of housewife as the lowest form of human endeavour, and put de facto relationships on the same level as married couples . . . It is time for the majority of people, both male and female to take on the radical feminists and re-introduce sanity to our society.

The same group, in a submission to the Australian Law Reform Commission, this time related to Matrimonial Property, stated:

Men should be given first consideration for custody of the children on the basis that they are more caring, better equipped for long-term planning and hence able to provide a more stable life for the children. Women on the other hand tend to be emotive, superficial and self-centred (Men's Confraternity, n.d.—1985?).

For these advocates, joint custody is seen not so much as a way of ensuring the 'welfare of the child' but as a means of continuing their control not only over their children, but also over their ex-wives. This campaign resonates with the general backlash against women and, in particular, against single mothers or, as some would call them, 'fatherless families'. In September 1987, the man named Queensland father of the year stated when accepting his award that children in 'fatherless families' ought to be adopted out, presumably into 'real' families. His remarks were, predictably, followed up by the then Queensland Welfare Minister, Mrs Lyn Chapman, in one of her characteristic attacks on single mothers. She urged compulsory sterilisation for the women, after their first child (ABC News 4 September 1987; *Courier Mail* 5 September 1987).

These attacks on 'fatherless' families and 'single parents' suggest that numerous women have children on their own so as to live a life of luxury on social security. In fact only a small fraction of 'single parents' started their parenting that way. It is clear from Department of Social Security data that the vast majority of female sole parents are the victims of a family structure (marriage, or de facto marriage) which has broken down (see Department of Social Security, 1988). Frequently, the breakdown follows a pattern of violence, yet community responses fail to make the connection between 'battered wives' for whom there is considerable sympathy, and 'single parents', the object of community opprobrium (see Graycar, 1988).

It is concern about the ideological resort to the terrain of 'the family', so evident in public discourses from election manifestos to the 'sole-parent bashing' documented above, which has led to reservations about the Child Support Scheme, and, in particular, its tendency to perpetuate (though mediated through state agencies) a continuing relationship between the adult parties after it has broken down (see, for example Kliger, 1988; Heron, 1987; Graycar, 1989a). Some women would rather forgo the extra few dollars per week child maintenance in order to avoid further contact, with the possibility of violence or harassment from their former partner. Whilst acknowledging that fathers should indeed be more responsible for their children, and, in particular, more financially responsible, it is some of the disturbing ideological aspects of the Child Support Scheme which have led feminist groups and welfare organisations to qualify their support for it. These arguments are too detailed to enumerate here,[4] but for present purposes the important connection is the similarity in the rhetoric used to promote joint custody and the way in which the Child Support Scheme resurrects the nuclear, albeit 'fissured', family. Both ideals presume the immutability of an 'eternal, biological family' (Sevenhuijsen, 1986: 336) even though for many people this does not represent the reality of their lives.

MATRIMONIAL PROPERTY

Another clear example of a resort to 'equality' rhetoric is provided by the 1980s debates about matrimonial property. Some feminists in Australia campaigned actively in favour of 'equal rights to marital assets'—specifically, the establishment of a community property regime (see, for example Scutt, 1983; Scutt and Graham, 1984). Detailed empirical work in the United States (see Weitzman, 1985), where community property is increasingly the norm, has shown that this form of equality is 'illusive' (see, for example, Fineman, 1983; 1986). Weitzman's work on the economic consequences of divorce for women and children is paralleled by research conducted by the Australian Institute of Family Studies (McDonald, 1986), which demonstrates that 'equal sharing' of marital assets may well leave women, with their limited access to the workforce and with the disadvantages accrued through years of child bearing and rearing, worse off. Women's post-divorce financial situation is dramatically worse than that of their husbands. The Institute of Family Studies demonstrated that after divorce, 78 per cent of women who had not repartnered were significantly worse off than before their divorce and 35 per cent were living below the poverty line (McDonald, 1986: 115–23; 311–12; Australian Law Reform Commission 1987b, paras 163–7).[5] This led the ALRC in its 1987 report on matrimonial property to eschew the rhetoric of equality in favour of a more realistic way of attempting to spread the economic disadvantages of divorce. Explicitly, they stated that a regime of equal sharing would leave women worse off than they already are (Australian Law Reform Commission, 1987b, para 273). They favoured 'practical, rather than formal equality', a distribution that would take account of and compensate women for their impaired capacity to achieve a reasonable standard of living, and for the responsibility for the children, still overwhelmingly falling on women in Australia (para 350). In a society where men and women are not equal, the ALRC correctly recognised that 'equal sharing' disadvantages women.

The purpose of this chapter has been to raise questions about the ways in which popular discourses, backed up by the enactment of anti-discrimination laws and reinforced by courts in a number of different contexts, tell us that women and men are now equal and that we live in a political and social environment characterised by equality. Moreover, the ideology of equality, historically so important to the campaigns of liberal feminism, has been garnered by conservative forces such as fathers' rights groups who crudely state that any time they don't 'win' custody, there is discrimination because of 'radical feminists' running the courts. At the same time as the men's demands for equality are being voiced, single parents have come under increasing attack, both in direct cuts to their living standards (nearly 90 per cent are dependent on Social Security, and benefits for single parents have been cut in a number of respects in recent years), and in rhetorical terms, such as the examples mentioned from Queensland, and from the Men's Confraternity in Western Australia. These phenomena signal a backlash against women, long before any of the gains women have sought in the public sphere have been significantly achieved. Ironically, even though women still overwhelmingly bear the responsibility for the care of children, disgruntled fathers see maternal custody as a sphere of 'success' for women which must be challenged on 'equality' grounds.

So far as custody is concerned, women should not have their children taken from them in the name of some 'illusive' equality. This is not to suggest that men who actually are involved in the day-to-day care of children should not have that recognised in case of a dispute after separation or divorce. A number of commentators have suggested that courts should adopt a 'primary carer principle' under which caretaking practices during the subsistence of a marriage would be given greater consideration by courts in custody disputes (see, for example Boyd, 1987; Fineman, 1988; Smart, 1989a). I am by no means proposing a return to notions of the innateness of motherhood, nor a resurrection of the 'tender years' doctrine. My purpose in this brief survey is simply to draw attention to the way in which somehow the practice of awarding women custody, in a cultural context where mothers are still overwhelmingly responsible for the day-to-day care of children, has been subjected to challenge by men in the name of 'equality' and 'discrimination'.

More generally, other examples such as the matrimonial property debate demonstrate that we should carefully scrutinise claims about 'equality' rather than presume that anything that wears that label is necessarily in the interests of women. Just as in the public sphere, formal equality has been recognised as able to do little, if anything, to redress endemic structural discrimination in employment, so also in the 'private sphere' we need to pay careful attention to the implications of notions such as 'joint custody' or 'equal rights to marital assets'.

5 Erratic bureaucracies: the intersection of housing, legal and social policies in the case of divorce

Housing discourses and practices operate within one distinctive arena, while legal discourses and practices occupy another. Rarely do the two intersect. Family law is no exception. In this chapter I shall examine how the Family Law Act 1975 (Cth) represents a locus of unacknowledged yet complex intersection. Most political or policy issues impact on several dimensions of individual and civil life, and most are the object of different policy arenas and discourses: the legal, the social, the financial or whatever. What is curious is that often each of these is treated as if it were unrelated, with different motivations and implications and with a different rhetoric. Within the context of the Family Law Act, there are separate, but related, policy arenas which intersect supposedly to assist (though often in fact to hinder) women on divorce. These are the housing system, the legal system, the income maintenance system and labour market policies.

Both the discourses and the intentions in these four areas are contradictory, resulting in a tangled web of disconnected policies and practices. Many women going through the divorce process fall into the interstices between these policies. Considering simply the policy level, one bureaucracy is divorced from another, with little interaction amongst the bureaucratic players to consider the mutual impact of their combined intentions. Negotiating the system is like negotiating Daedalus' labyrinth. You need to unwind a thread to find your way back.

If the state is understood in Foucauldian terms with no assumption of a unity, autonomy or definitive functionality, we would not expect to find coherence in its policies. Instead, Foucault shifts the focus to an analysis of power which does not

> look for the headquarters that presides over its rationality, neither the caste which governs, nor the groups which control the state apparatus, nor those who make the most important economic decisions which direct the entire network of power that functions in a society (and makes it function); the rationality of power is characterized by tactics which, becoming connected to one another, but finding their base of support and their condition elsewhere, end by forming comprehensive systems (Foucault, 1979: 95).

Rather than focus on the whole field of actual power relations, of which the state occupies no more than a part (Foucault 1980: 122), I shall look at the apparatuses of the state and their disunified effects in the constitution of housing policies for divorced women.

HOUSING IN AUSTRALIA

There are at least two relevant foci to housing discourses in Australia: the notion of individual free choice and the notion of the traditional patriarchal family. The first implies primarily private consumption. In Australia, there is a pervasive ideology of individual home ownership, which is presumed to constitute a natural desire, even an instinct. Everyone can do it. Even if governments have to provide some form of subsidy or assistance, it is simply a question of choosing the right house in the right location and proceeding with the purchase. The second underlying ideological notion is equally pernicious. Home ownership helps to create, produce and reproduce specific patriarchal familial relations. Discourses of the home as a man's castle have been important in shaping the form that policies have taken. Illustrations from the debates in the Senate or House of Representatives over the last century are legion:

> A man whose home is his own has the satisfaction of knowing that every tree that he plants in the garden, every cupboard that he installs, every improvement that he makes, is his own. That is the attitude of almost every man worthy of his family (Hansard, Senate, 4 October 1945, Volume 185: 6455).

Notions of nation, masculinity, citizenship and home ownership combine to construct women as the protected (the prisoner), the dependent and the marginal.

> The safety of this country, like the safety of all other countries, depends on private home ownership which gives a man a stake in the country. A place of his own in which to keep his wife and rear a

family, and a place for his family to live when he dies (Hansard, House of Representatives, 3 October 1945, Volume 185: 6355).

This extract comes from the debate on the first Commonwealth-State Housing Agreement in 1945, which set the scene for Commonwealth housing policies in the postwar years.

Federal and state housing policies have favoured the nuclear family household at both a direct and an indirect level. That is, some policies have specifically excluded from assistance certain forms of household, for example single-parent families or single people, and instead have favoured others. In addition, other policies have indirectly excluded women as gendered subjects by directing the major component of government housing expenditure towards home ownership, from which women are marginalised as a result of their economic position as well as discriminatory practices in the workplace and in the policies of financial institutions (Watson, 1988: 39–56). Thus, a much greater proportion of overall federal and state housing expenditure in Australia has been directed at the patriarchal nuclear family household. It follows that, for a woman, her only route to home ownership, the most privileged form of tenure, may be to find and depend upon a male partner. For reasons of income and employment status, and financial institutions' discriminatory practices, she could not otherwise reach this mecca. A statistical profile of the ownership rates of different forms of household substantiates my argument. Forty-six per cent of female single parents, compared to 61 per cent of male single parents and 75 per cent of men in two-parent families with dependent children were owning or purchasing their dwellings in 1981 (Watson, 1988: 43).

Given this picture, we could pose the question—why do so many women divorce when they run the risk of losing their accommodation or becoming homeless? The question is all the more valid in light of the Institute of Family Studies' evidence that women are more likely to initiate the separation than their male partners (McDonald, 1986), demonstrating that women do not tend to be the passive victims of another's decision. The answer, though speculative, is that probably many more women would divorce if more affordable housing were available. Supply defines demand which is often taken as an inaccurate measure of overall need, rather than as simply an indication of the level of expressed need. In Japan, where levels of divorce are very low, it is widely recognised that this does not so much reflect high levels of marital harmony as low female labour force participation, very high land and house prices and a scarcity of low-cost rental accommodation.

HOUSING AFTER DIVORCE

Before examining the recent changes to the social security legislation and their intersection with housing, the labour market, and legal arenas, the housing context needs elaborating. Housing is clearly a major component in the well-being of newly formed households after divorce. This is particularly so where children are involved. Unlike some commodities and financial assets, the problem with a dwelling is that it cannot be divided into two. The issue then is how to formulate policies which enable both households to be accommodated as opposed to leaving both or one household homeless. Available evidence suggests that the current housing system is far from coping well with marital breakdown, and is too inflexible to accommodate the changing social, demographic and economic trends. The staggering number of single parents on the public housing waiting lists, which is growing every year, is one measure of the extent of the problem. In New South Wales, for example, the number of new applicants for public housing increased from 25 331 in 1979/80 to 31 763 in 1985/86, of which approximately one-third were single parents (Watson, 1988: 13, 92).

What are the options for individuals and their dependants on divorce? As stated earlier, the majority form of tenure in Australia is home ownership. In Australia approximately 70 per cent of all households are owners or purchasers, 15 per cent are private tenants and 5 per cent public tenants (ABS, 1986). Marital breakdown has different implications for the household, depending on the form of tenure in which they live. It is important first to note that in nine cases out of ten (McDonald, 1986) it is the women who take the major responsibility for care of the children on divorce. If the household were public tenants, and the man leaves the woman and children, she retains the tenancy. If she wants to transfer to another tenancy due to fear of her partner's violence, or out of a desire for anonymity, she may have to wait for a considerable period of time. Policies on transfers vary between states, with some housing authorities (for example the Northern Territory) requiring that the legal custody of the children is finalised before an alternative is offered, while others (for example the South Australian Housing Trust) will offer interim accommodation, provided it is relinquished if the husband obtains custody.

If the woman leaves the tenancy with her children, or applies for public housing from another tenure, unless the household is considered to be a priority case, in which case accommodation may be offered quickly, they will be subject to the same waiting period as all new applicants. This may be a period of up to five years, with great variation within regions and between states. Considerable pressure on a small public housing sector and increasing levels of homelessness and unemployment has meant that more and more applicants could be defined as priority cases. This has had the effect in some states of making the priority category either inoperable or more and more narrow. Thus a battered woman with health problems, five children, and living in a temporary refuge could well find herself ineligible for priority housing.

The non-custodial spouse who leaves the tenancy or an individual who leaves the dwelling with no dependent children under eighteen, and applies for public housing either as a former public tenant or from another tenure, is in an even worse situation. The orientation of public housing towards family households has meant that single households have been ineligible for accommodation in most states. (South Australia and the Australian Capital Territory are notable exceptions). More recently, Victoria and New South Wales have initiated singles housing policies, but accommodation is scarce and often unsuitable since it is shared. This lack of housing for individuals on their own disadvantages women, particularly those who are dependent on the provision of low cost accommodation on account of their lower incomes. In May 1987, female average total weekly earnings were 65 per cent of male average total weekly earnings (ABS, 1987). Homelessness then is not an uncommon experience for women on marital breakdown, particularly where no dependent children are involved (Watson, 1986).

Marital breakdown for those in the private rental sector is a less complex issue. If the woman is left in the tenancy, the landlord will usually transfer the tenancy into her name, so long as the rental payments are guaranteed. If, however, a woman leaves with her children and has to find private rented accommodation, her chances of finding secure, low cost, adequate accommodation are slight. First, there is evidence of discrimination towards single parents from landlords and real estate agents (Watson and Coleman, 1986). Second, the scarcity of rental accommodation and high levels of demand in the major cities have led to rents that are prohibitive to many women.

Home ownership is the most significant form of tenure, not simply at a numerical level, but because it represents the largest financial asset of most couples going through the divorce process (McDonald, 1986). For this reason, the legal response to property division is crucial. In Australia, the Family Law Act 1975 (Cth) permits all the property of the spouses, however and wherever acquired, to be divided on marriage breakdown. The discretion of the judges of the Family Court is fairly considerable (see Family Law Act, s.79), although broadly speaking the judge will weigh up the contributions to the property against the future needs of the spouses. Contributions include both financial (usually the husband's) and domestic (usually the wife's), and a dilemma obviously arises over the relative worth of each. This Act has been the subject of some debate within feminist circles. Scutt and Graham (1984) argue that married women would be better off with a joint property arrangement with their husbands during marriage, and fixed equal sharing of property on divorce. But as Shiff and others have pointed out, there are several problems with their proposals. Shiff and McIllhatton argue:

> Joint management would symbiotically tie each spouse to the other so that neither would engage in commercial dealings without the agreement of the other . . . [Secondly it] may rebound dangerously against women, subjecting their financial independence to their husband's control . . . [Thirdly, [Scutt and Graham's]] proposal assumes unity of property between husband and wife in which each shares in the income of the other (Shiff and McIllhatton, 1985: 29, 30).

This runs counter to feminist campaigns to have the state treat a woman as separate from her husband for the purposes of tax and social security entitlement. Moreover, there is no evidence to suggest, as Scutt and Graham (1984) assert, that divorced women would be better off with a fixed property rights regime in which they were automatically entitled to equal shares. Indeed American research suggests that lower income wives are worse off when they are subject to an equal sharing of debts and liabilities on divorce (Watson and Shiff, 1984). And Lenore Weitzman's central study of the economic effects of divorce on women and children in California demonstrates that a fixed, equal-sharing regime often results in the sale of the home, leaving women and children with inadequate financial resources to rehouse (Weitzman, 1985).

In my view a discretionary based system of matrimonial property division is the most appropriate model. In the first place, a discretionary system provides a mechanism for compensating for the inequalities between men and women, many of which derive from marriage. Women are more likely to suffer adverse consequences and have greater needs than men on divorce, are less likely than men to be well qualified or trained or to have secure and well-paid employment and are likely to have poorer employment prospects than men. These disadvantages derive from both their former role within the marriage as mothers and housewives and from the sex-segmented nature of the labour market and women's 'inferior' position in society generally. Moreover, women are far more likely than men to have the custody of the children on divorce (McDonald, 1986).

Obviously this is not a uniform picture; women's income status and employment prospects vary according to age, race and background; so also do housing prospects. Moreover, there are obviously cases where women's employment prospects and income are better than their husbands' and where men gain the custody of the children. More commonly though, women's economic position disadvantages them either in their access to new mortgages on divorce or in buying out their husband's share of the matrimonial home, or in sustaining high levels of ongoing mortgage repayments. When the discrimination that women suffer from financial institutions is added to the picture, the situation can be dire. While there is a discrepancy between the two partners' needs and prospects (where usually women are worse off), and in particular their housing needs and prospects, a discretionary system of property allocation can help alleviate the inequitable outcomes on divorce. Significantly, the Family Law Act gives the Family Court important powers, through the use of its discretion under s.79, to reallocate property, notwithstanding formal legal rules about ownership.

A second and related point is that variations in housing markets and housing policies between states mean that equal division of matrimonial property has a differential effect depending on where the couple lived. If we take the example of a property settlement between two parties who have previously had state concessional home loans in the Northern Territory and South Australia, where the woman has custody of the children and has no employment and the man has a low income, different shares may be appropriate. In the Northern Territory, neither party is eligible for another concessional loan, house prices are high, waiting periods for public sector housing are long, and single applicants (who are not government employees) are unlikely to be accepted. Under these circumstances the court might allocate the matrimonial home in its entirety to the woman, in the recognition that there is no housing alternative for her and the children. Alternatively, it may decide to give an order for occupation of the marital home until the children are no longer dependent, or until the woman has found employment and possible private home loan finance. Or, it may decide that awarding the entire housing equity to the woman is not fair, since the male partner also has few housing options, and may therefore look towards a more even distribution. In the context of such a decision, it could be argued that the marginal effects of awarding the woman a slightly greater share are small, since in any event she will be unable to repurchase. The court may thus decide on a strict fifty-fifty division as the fairest option.

In contrast, in South Australia, both parties will be eligible for a state concessional loan despite the fact that the woman is in receipt of sole parent pension and the man is a single householder. Further, both new households will have access to public housing within a shorter period than they would in the Northern Territory. Thus the judge may award equal shares in the recognition that both parties have a 'relatively' equal chance of obtaining further accommodation, or may decide, for example, that the age of the woman concerned warrants her receiving a slightly greater share of the equity to enable her to be assisted more easily by the state home-purchase scheme. Under such circumstances, it would probably be inappropriate either to give an order for a long period of occupation or to award the entire matrimonial home to the custodial parent.

These snapshots serve simply as illustrations of the importance of taking into account state variations in housing markets and housing policies in matrimonial property division, an area subject to a national family law regime. In reality every situation is different and often more complex. The argument is that such state variation points to the importance of a discretionary system of matrimonial property division, until there is more uniformity in housing provision and housing policies across Australia. This is particularly the case where women are concerned.

The Institute of Family Studies undertook a study for the Australian Law Reform Commission's Matrimonial Property Inquiry of several hundred couples who had gone through the Family Court process. From data collected on the disposition of the marital homes, it was found that the house was sold in approximately 35 per cent of cases, transferred to the wife in about 35 per cent of cases and transferred to the husband in about 20 per cent of cases. In the remaining 10 per cent, ownership of the house was unchanged (McDonald, 1986: Chapter 8). The tendency was for the house to be sold when the mortgage was high and the equity low, or when the house had a very high value.

Overall, 40 per cent of those surveyed had dropped out of home ownership where the house was sold or the other spouse remained in the marital home. Given the upper socioeconomic bias of the sample, it is likely that at a national level the percentage would be higher (McDonald, 1986: 164). There was also a direct relationship between who stayed in the home after the separation and who was allocated the home on settlement: 94 per cent of the women who remained in the house for the three months after separation received the dwelling as part of the final property allocation. The final points of interest are that a much higher proportion of men repartnered, a factor which has implications for their ease of access to new joint mortgages. Second, women tended to be paying higher housing costs than men at the time of the interview. Fifty-six percent of those interviewed were paying more than one quarter of their income on their accommodation.

What is the relevance of these findings? In at least a third of cases women are managing to retain the marital home. Even if their repayments are high, they have a roof over their heads for themselves and their children. This is important since once women lose the home their access to alternative housing is limited. It is also important because it means that less disruption has been caused to their own and their childrens' social, community and educational networks. It appears, therefore, that the Family Law Act has operated as a useful mechanism in providing housing for a large number of women on divorce. To return to my earlier point concerning the disconnections between, and unintended impacts of, the policy arenas, the discretionary features of the Act may also be important in redressing the great disparities between states in housing policy terms. These merits have been both obscured and unintentional.

LEGISLATIVE CHANGES

The 1987 amendments to the Family Law Act and the related changes to the Social Security legislation (connected with the establishment of the Commonwealth Child Support Scheme) are likely to have an adverse effect on this outcome. Under the Family Law Act the amount of capital or housing equity transferred under the settlement as part of the maintenance arrangements has to be specified. Under the corresponding Social Security legislation, this equity is imputed as income and subject to a special maintenance income test. There are several implications here. First, women who have received the marital home as part of the maintenance settlement will be liable to a reduction in their benefit (though in cases of housing maintenance, the maximum level of reduction is 25 per cent). This will mean that mortgage repayments will have to be met from a reduced pension, pushing women further into poverty. Given that the proportion of income that women spend on mortgage repayments is already considerably higher than their male counterparts, women may well be forced to sell the dwelling and move out of home ownership.

This scenario brings me back to the argument raised earlier, that is the lack of connections made between different policy areas in terms of the discourses used, the policy intentions embedded, and the outcomes of the policies. Central to the social security changes is the notion that women's dependence on the state for income support should be reduced. Instead, women will be encouraged to enter labour market training programmes, enter the workforce and support themselves. In principle, the objective appears a sensible one.

In reality, however, if a woman sells up her marital home in Sydney she has three options: to trade down in the housing market, to enter the public sector where stocks are scarce, or to enter the increasingly restricted private rental sector. The first two options may well imply moving out west where land and house prices are cheaper and where the majority of Department of Housing dwellings are located. These are precisely the same areas where there are high levels of female unemployment, particularly amongst single parents. The accessibility of employment, and transport problems (to introduce yet another disconnected and distinct policy area), also operate as significant constraints. Whether labour market training programmes will go to these areas is anyone's guess.

The move to subject housing equity, transferred as maintenance, to an income test may well, in the long run, lead to unintended, contradictory and unwanted consequences. Women's marginal income and employment status will once again be reinforced. The combined effects of housing markets and labour markets could well lead to *increased* dependence on the state for income support through lack of employment opportunities. The maintenance income test is anomalous within the social security system, since under general means-testing policies, the principal home is usually exempt from assets testing. Even within this one policy area we see contradictions, although these contradictions should be no surprise if we accept a more fragmented and erratic view of the state, and the discourses and arenas which constitute it. In addition, the policies are based on the notion that the major players—the solicitors, the DSS pensions officers and so on— have a rational understanding of both the means tests and the housing system. Such an assumption is clearly false. At the time of writing, the effects of this legislation can only be a matter for conjecture as it has been in force only since mid-1988.

I want to conclude this chapter at two levels. First, at the pragmatic level, it is clear from the evidence presented here that women in general, particularly women with children, have limited options for re-establishing and rehousing themselves on divorce. Since 1975, economic disadvantages accrued through marriage appear to have been somewhat ameliorated through the discretionary system of property allocation in the Family Law Act. The 1987 amendments to the Family Law Act and the new Social Security legislation can only worsen what are already, for many women, the dire consequences of marriage and divorce in a country where home ownership is the major housing option. Second, this examination of women's housing options after divorce has illustrated how several different policy arenas and discourses, which constitute the state, intersect in complex and often unexpected and unintended ways. It is women who are frequently caught in the centre of this confused morass, locked into shifting dependencies on men or the various agencies of the state.

MARY JANE MOSSMAN

6 Women lawyers in twentieth century Canada: rethinking the image of 'Portia'

I think all lawyers must agree
On keeping our profession free
From females whose admission would
Result in anything but good.
Because it yet has to be shown
That men are fit to hold their own
In such a contest, I've no doubt
We'd some of us be crowded out.
(Grip, 1892; quoted in Mullins, 1986)

These words were written five years before Clara Brett Martin, the first woman to become a lawyer in the British Commonwealth, was admitted to the legal profession in Ontario. Her admission as a barrister and solicitor in Ontario was initially thwarted by the Law Society of Upper Canada, and was finally accomplished only as a result of legislative amendments expressly authorising the admission of women as lawyers (Backhouse, 1985).[1] At the time of her call to the Bar in 1897, the Canada Law Journal published its congratulations and wished her success in her chosen profession, but also expressed the editors' fervent hope 'that she [might] be the one brilliant exception to the time-honoured rule which has hitherto closed our ranks to those who are not of the male persuasion' (Canada Law Journal, 1897: 133).

Such sentiments were widely shared by legal commentators at the turn of the century (Backhouse, 1985: 8–9). Moreover, in the two decades after Clara Brett Martin's admission as a lawyer, only a small number of other women were admitted to the legal profession in Ontario, leading one observer to comment that 'the admission of women to the practice of law has had in Ontario no effect upon the Bar or the Courts; the public and all concerned regard it with indifference' (Riddell, 1918: 205). In the same period, however, the issue of the admission of women to the legal profession was litigated in the courts in three other Canadian provinces: New Brunswick, British Columbia and Quebec. The judicial decisions in these cases, all denying women's claims to enter the legal profession, offer important insights concerning our ideas about sex roles for women and men, both then and now. These three cases are also interesting examples of efforts to use litigation to focus issues of legal and social change for women in the twentieth century.

According to the records of The Law Society of Upper Canada, eight women had been admitted as lawyers prior to 1918, and three more were admitted in that year. Legislative amendments permitted women to become lawyers in Alberta and Manitoba in 1915, in Saskatchewan in 1917, in Nova Scotia in 1918, in Prince Edward Island in 1926, and in Newfoundland in 1933 (Harvey, 1970).

In these years, women were also admitted to the legal professions in Australia and New Zealand. Between 1903 when Victoria removed the legal barrier preventing women from entering the legal profession and 1923 when Western Australia did so, all the states of Australia changed their legislative provisions to enable women to become lawyers (Weisbrot, 1988: 270). In New Zealand, there was no woman lawyer until 1901, and the first to practise law independently, Ellen Melville, opened her office in Auckland in 1909 (Murray, 1988: 329).

This chapter explores some of the issues debated in the Canadian cases concerning women's right to practise law in the first two decades of this century, and the pervasive influence of the history of women lawyers on their current status in the legal profession. Also examined is the impact of ever-increasing numbers of women lawyers in the legal profession in recent years, focusing especially on efforts to confront the 'maleness' of law in the legal education process (O'Brien and McIntyre, 1986: 69). While recognising the significant changes which have occurred for women lawyers, the chapter also documents the need for further reforms, and begins to explore the ways in which changes occur in the acceptable roles for women and men in our society. Just as the idea of 'separate spheres' for women and men at the turn of the century—so well-illustrated both in the words of the anonymous poet quoted above and in the judicial opinions in the admission cases—affected the options available to women lawyers then, so similar ideas about law and the legal process affect our understanding of current issues for both women and men who are lawyers (Mossman, 1988).

'SEPARATE SPHERES' AND WOMEN AS LAWYERS

Mabel Penury French was the applicant in the first Canadian case, litigated in New Brunswick (*In re French*, 1906). She graduated from King's College Law School in Saint John with a Bachelor of Civil Law degree in June 1905, having led her classes, and then articled with the firm of Bustin and Porter (Mullins, 1986: 676). When her application for admission as a lawyer was considered by the New Brunswick Barristers' Society, the Society passed a formal resolution recommending her admission, 'subject to the opinion of the court as to her sex being under existing laws a bar to her admission' (*In re French*, 1906 at 359). The Society had concluded that a judicial opinion was needed to determine whether women were included in the word 'persons' in the *Barristers' Society Act* since the Act authorised the Society to regulate 'the admission of persons to the study of law' (*Barristers' Society Act*, 1903: section 13).

Ms French was ably represented in the court challenge by three well established lawyers, all of whom staunchly supported an interpretation of the legislation which would have included women as 'persons'. One of the lawyers suggested forcefully that:

> The trend of recent legislation, both political and judicial, is to remove the disabilities of women and open to them every avenue leading to avocations which may enable them to earn a livelihood. Why delve into the dark ages for a precedent to justify holding them incompetent or by law disqualified from exercising a calling to which we have every reason to believe, from their successes in our universities and in the professions which have been opened to them, they will bring to bear equal intelligence, greater diligence and devotion to duty than men? (*In re French*, 1906 at 360–1).

It appears that Ms French also had considerable support outside the court. For example, the provincial Attorney General, William Pugsley asserted, that 'Women possess the natural right to admission to one of the noblest callings in the land.' He continued:

> Others may hold that women's sphere is the domestic circle. That might carry force were all provided with happy comforable homes, but when we find them driven out by stress of circumstances to earn their livelihood in the busy walks of life, and find them doing so with honour and credit to themselves, why should a man stand up and say they shall not engage in the practice of law? They have entered our universities and fought their way to the front ranks against the competition of our brightest sons (Mullins, 1986: 677).

The five judges who heard the case, however, were not persuaded that the word 'persons' in the Barristers' Society Act included women. Mr Justice Tuck dismissed the arguments based on 'the advanced thought of the age and the right of women to share with men in all paying public activities', and concluded that the word 'persons' in the statute included only men since 'it was never in the contemplation of the legislature that a woman should be admitted an attorney of this court' (*In re French*, 1906 at 361–2). Mr Justice Barker agreed, dismissing the suggestion that there was any right at common law for women to become lawyers and enthusiastically adopting the idea of 'separate spheres'[2] for men and women 'founded in the divine ordinance as well as in the nature of things' (*In re French*, 1906 at 365–6). He also agreed with Mr Justice Tuck that the statute's use of the word 'persons' could not have been intended to include women because no women were lawyers when the statute was first enacted in 1846, and it was clear therefore that the statute had never been intended to make 'the radical change' suggested by Ms French's application (*In re French*, 1906 at 371). Unanimously, the court concluded that women could not be admitted to the legal profession in New Brunswick.

Ms French was subsequently admitted as a lawyer in New Brunswick when, later in 1906, the provincial legislature enacted the *Act to Remove the Disability of Women so far as Relates to the Study and Practice of the Law*. The Act provided for the admission of women 'upon the same terms, and subject to the like conditions and regulations as men' in section 1, and gave retrospective approval to any women admitted to the study of law prior to the enactment of the legislation in section 2; presumably, the latter section was required to admit Ms French. The Act was apparently introduced to the legislature and supported by William Pugsley, the Attorney General (Mullins, 1986: 677).

After a number of years of legal practice in New Brunswick, however, Ms French moved to Vancouver in 1910 where she worked in the firm established there by her friend Joseph Russell (Mullins, 1986: 677). At that time, there were no women lawyers in British Columbia, and the provincial Law Society had privately expressed its satisfaction with this state of affairs in a letter to an Ontario lawyer:

> In reply to your enquiry of the 10th instant, I beg to say that the fair sex have not yet threatened to invade the legal profession in British Columbia. Their efforts so far have been confined to the trials of suffragettes in Municipal elections, or else they consider that their interests are fully protected by the male sex so far as forensic science is concerned. The Benchers not yet having to consider the legislation of a modern Blackstone in petticoats to enter the profession it is difficult to say what their feelings would be or what decision they would reach

when the moment of decision arises (*The Advocate*, 1970: 270; quoting letter 1908).

The moment of decision arose when Ms French submitted her application to write the exams for admission to the legal profession in British Columbia in 1911.

Initially, the Law Society failed to acknowledge her application. However after a submission by a senior partner in the firm where she was employed, the Benchers considered her application and denied permission to write the exams on the basis that the legislation in British Columbia, like that formerly in place in New Brunswick and Ontario, did not authorise them to admit women as lawyers (Mullins, 1986: 677). The Law Society's decision reflected the opinions of a majority of the Benchers, but there were two dissenters, Sir Charles Hibbert Tupper, K.C. and J.H. Senkler, K.C. The Secretary of the Law Society also remarked privately that Ms French's application was 'apparently taken more out of a spirit of advertising rather than with any hope of success' (Mullins, 1986: 677). Ms French then sought the court's opinion as to the correctness of the Benchers' decision in an application for a writ of mandamus.[3]

At the initial hearing, counsel for the Law Society argued that there was no common law right for women to be admitted to the legal profession and that the use of the word 'persons' in s.37 of the *Legal Professions Act* 1897 (British Columbia) did not include women, citing *In re French* in New Brunswick as legal authority for both these arguments (*Re French*, 1911 at 2–3). Mr Russell argued on behalf of Ms French's application, however, that the word 'persons' was broad enough to include women as well as men,[4] and that Ms French was entitled to be admitted under the provisions permitting the admission of duly qualified barristers and solicitors from other Canadian provinces as well as on her own merits (*Re French*, 1911 at 1–2). However, Mr Justice Morrison concluded that Ms French's application could not succeed because 'the Legislature had not in mind the contingency that women would invoke the provisions of the Act'; and suggested that 'her only remedy [was] by way of aid from the Legislature, before a committee of which, doubtless, Mr Russell's gallant argument [might] prevail' (*Re French*, 1911 at 3–4).

The British Columbia Court of Appeal unanimously dismissed an appeal by Ms French. According to Chief Justice MacDonald, the 'trend of authority at common law [was] that women [were] not eligible' for admission as lawyers (*Re French*, 1912 at 4), citing in particular the 1873 United States Supreme Court decision of *Bradwell v Illinois*. Moreover, even if there were 'cogent reasons for a change based upon changes in the legal status of women, . . . [the court would be] usurping the functions of the Legislature rather than discharging the duty of the Court, which is to decide what the law is, not what it ought to be' (*Re French*, 1912 at 4–5). Mr Justice Irving agreed with the Chief Justice, referring as well to the absence of women in the legal profession in England:

> To my mind, . . . this fact that no woman has ever been admitted in England, is conclusive that the word 'person' in our own Act was not intended to include a woman. The context of our Act refers to a profession for men, and men alone (*Re French*, 1912 at 6).

Following the court's decision, Ms French continued to work in the Vancouver law firm where she was employed, and the firm continued to support her claim for admission to the legal profession. Eventually, she obtained the assistance of Evlyn Farris, the President of the University Women's Club and 'a strong advocate of women's rights'. With the help of editorial support from the local newspapers, Mrs Farris was able to persuade the Attorney General, William Bowser, to introduce legislation to permit women to become lawyers in British Columbia (Mullins, 1986: 678; Pazdro, 1980: 17). Having passed her examinations, Mabel Penury French was called to the Bar of British Columbia. The minutes of the Benchers recorded that on 1 April 1912 'twenty gentlemen, including Mabel Penury French' were admitted as lawyers (Watts, 1984: 134).

Meanwhile, in England, the issue of the admission of women as lawyers had been raised a number of times during the two decades after Clara Brett Martin's admission to the legal profession in Ontario. In *Hall v Incorp. Society of Law Agents* (1901), a Scottish court decided that women were not eligible to become law agents, and in 1903, the Benchers of Gray's Inn denied Bertha Cave's application to join the Inn as a barrister. In *Bebb v Law Society* (1913), the English Chancery Court concluded that a woman could not be admitted as a solicitor, notwithstanding the use of the word 'persons' in the relevant statute (Sachs and Hoff Wilson, 1978: 27–8).

In Quebec, the third case concerned Annie Macdonald Langstaff (*Langstaff v Bar of Quebec*, 1915). She grew up in Ontario but later moved to Montreal. After separating from her husband, she supported herself and her daughter by working for the law firm of Jacobs, Hall and Garneau. In 1911, with the encouragement of her employers, she entered the Faculty of Law at McGill University where she became the first woman to graduate in 1914, achieving first-class honours and an overall class standing of fourth place (Gillet, 1981: 309; Morgentaler, 1984: 20–1; Baines, 1988: 157). The board of examiners refused to permit her to take the examination preliminary to becoming a student-at-law, and she then issued a writ of mandamus to compel them to allow her to do so.

The Bar of Quebec 'strenuously' opposed Ms Langstaff's application on a number of grounds, including her status as a married woman. In the initial hearing, Mr Justice Saint-Pierre decided that the use of masculine pronouns in the legislation could not be interpreted so as to include women in the absence of proof of intent to do so on the part of the legislature, and he cited both English and French authorities to support his conclusion (*Langstaff v Bar of Quebec*, 1915 at 143). In denying the application, Mr Justice Saint-Pierre expressed the hope that 'her ambition in life should be directed towards the seeking of a field of labor more suitable to the sex and more likely to ensure for her the success in life to which her irreprocheable (sic) conduct and remarkable talents [gave] her the right to aspire' (*Langstaff v Bar of Quebec*, 1915 at 145).

A majority of judges decided to dismiss her appeal. The Chief Justice suggested that the absence of any women admitted to the Bar of Quebec itself demonstrated that there was no legislative intent to include women in the interpretation of eligibility requirements for the practice of law (*Langstaff v Bar of Quebec*, 1916 at 20). However, one of the appeal judges, Mr Justice Lavergne, dissented. Focusing exclusively on the words of the Civil Code, he concluded that the fact that the law stated expressly that women could not be notaries, could not be elected to Parliament, and could not serve on juries meant that the legislature's failure to prohibit women (expressly) from becoming members of the legal profession signified an intent to permit them to do so:

> Le candidat à l'étude du droit peut être ou du sexe masculin ou du sexe féminin sans distinction . . . Si le législateur avait voulu dire qu'une femme ne pourrait être avocat, il l'aurait dit (*Langstaff v Bar of Quebec*, 1916 at 13–14).

As in the other provinces, efforts were made to achieve legislative recognition for women lawyers in Quebec as well, and Mr Jacobs, the lawyer who had argued both cases on behalf of Ms Langstaff, prepared a legislative amendment for submission to the Quebec Legislative Assembly. Unfortunately, the proposed amendment was defeated, and it was not until 1941 that Quebec legislation permitted women to practise law (Gillet, 1981: 309; Morgentaler, 1984: 21; Baines, 1988: 163).

Annie Macdonald Langstaff continued to work at the law firm until 1965 when, at the age of 78, she retired. When the legislative amendment was passed in 1941, she was still ineligible for admission to the legal profession because it required eligible candidates to have both an undergraduate degree and a law degree, and she had only a law degree. When she died ten years after her retirement, she had never been admitted to the legal profession of Quebec (Morgentaler, 1984: 21).

Langstaff v Bar of Quebec is significant because it reinforced the idea of 'separate spheres' for women and men, illustrated a decade earlier in 1906 in the judgment of Mr Justice Barker in *In re French*. In the initial hearing before Mr Justice Saint-Pierre in Ms Langstaff's case, the judge explained succinctly why it was improper for women to practise law:

> A woman may be as brave as any man, and scenes which are in the present time, daily depicted to us, show that many of them are proving their usefulness as nurses on the field of battle; but the physical constitution of a woman makes it plain that nature never intended her to take part along with the stronger sex in the bloody affrays of the battle field . . .

> I would put within the range of possibilities though by no means a commendable one, the admission of a woman to the profession of *avoué*, but I hold that to admit a woman and more particularly a married woman as a *barrister*, that is to say, as a *person who pleads cases at the bar before judges or juries in open court and in the presence of the public*, would be nothing short of a direct infringement upon public order and a manifest violation of the law of good morals and public decency (*Langstaff v Bar of Quebec*, 1915 at 139 [emphasis in original]).

Despite the judge's recognition of work being done by women in World War I, his comments reflect his understanding of such efforts as both exceptional and undesirable except under extremely abnormal circumstances. Moreover, his views about the impropriety of women engaging in such work clearly demonstrate his acceptance of the 'separate spheres' doctrine, even in the face of evidence that women were able to do work previously undertaken only by men. It was not a matter of women's capacity for 'men's' work, but rather one of the propriety of women doing it.

Indeed, it is these ideas about differentiated gender roles which provide the key to understanding the consistently negative outcomes in these three cases about the admission of women to the legal profession. Nothing in law compelled the judges hearing these cases to reach the conclusions they did (Mossman, 1986; 1987). When the *French* cases were decided in both New Brunswick and British Columbia, for example, there was no precedent which required judges to conclude that women could not practise as lawyers. Similarly, there was no legal precedent which required them to conclude that their respective legislatures, in using the gender-neutral word 'persons', intended to include only male persons. By the time of the *Langstaff* decision, of course, there was an English decision (Bebb v Law Society 1913, at 634) but it was not binding in the province of Quebec. Moreover, as was demonstrated by the dissent of Mr Justice Lavergne in the Quebec Court of Appeal, there was an equally compelling interpretation of the statutory language which no other judge chose to accept. In the absence of legal precedents requiring a negative outcome, and in the context of other arguments which were equally acceptable in law, what explanation can be offered for these judicial choices?

The idea of 'separate spheres', referred to expressly in the *French* case in New Brunswick and implicitly in the *Langstaff* decision in Quebec, offers a way of understanding the outcome of these cases. In early twentieth-century Canada, the idea of 'separate spheres' created the public world of work for men and the private world of the family for women (Cook and Mitchinson, 1976). In this context, the idea of 'lawyer' was male, both in terms of legal theory and in the ideas of most members of society. Since women were not males, it followed that they could not be lawyers. Indeed, the amending legislation enacted after the *French* cases in New Brunswick and British Columbia, which provided for the admission of women as lawyers 'on the same terms as men', expressly recognised a male standard of lawyering.[5] By accepting maleness as the standard for being a lawyer, moreover, women who became lawyers did so on the understanding that their acceptance as lawyers depended on their conformity to such a standard. In this respect, the admission of women to the legal profession in Canada challenged its exclusivity for men, but not its male exclusivity. And this legacy—the standard of maleness in the law, in the process of lawyering, and in legal education—presents a formidable and continuing challenge for women who are lawyers at the end of the twentieth century.

THE 'FEMINISATION' OF THE LEGAL PROFESSION

The difficulties experienced by Clara Brett Martin, Mabel Penury French and Annie Macdonald Langstaff in gaining admission to the legal profession in Canada seem remote for many women lawyers in the 1980s. Although the numbers of women entering the legal profession were initially small (Harvey, 1970), 'the change in the last two decades is nothing short of revolutionary' (Abel, 1988: 202),[6] leading many to conclude that there are no remaining problems for women as lawyers. By 1987, for example, women lawyers in Ontario represented 18.6 per cent of the total number of lawyers in the province, an astonishing increase over the proportion a decade earlier when women represented only about 5 per cent of the total number of members of the legal profession in the province (Burnett, 1977: 71–3). An even more significant numbers 'revolution' has occurred in Canadian law schools where the numbers of women, which had 'remained miniscule until about 1970' (Arthurs et al., 1988), zoomed to nearly 50 per cent in the past two decades.

Similar increases in the proportion of women law students have occurred elsewhere, including in Australia, where women now constitute 40–50 per cent of the total student population in university law schools (Weisbrot, 1988: 270–1). Yet, the achievement of numerical equality for women and men in the legal profession and in the law schools has already been identified as only one part of the 'revolution':

> To acknowledge that increasing numbers of women in law schools is important in shaping attitudes toward the profession is not to suggest that numbers alone are sufficient. Numbers are only a start; they are *necessary* to begin to affect attitudes, but they are not *sufficient* . . . The increasing numbers of women have had little impact on the pervasiveness of gender bias in the profession. And despite the statistical increase in women students and faculty, gender bias in legal education persists (Schneider, 1988: 89 [emphasis in original]).[7]

For Schneider and others in the United States context, there is an urgent need for law schools to assess the content of the curriculum and the casebooks (the major law school teaching tool), the dynamics of the classroom, and the 'neutrality' of scholarship to 'remedy the problems' identified in a number of state-sponsored task force reports on gender bias in the legal system. 'The law schools will be successful only when all law school graduates are not only knowledgeable about and sensitive to women's concerns in the law but have eradicated gender bias in their own practice' (Schneider, 1988: 95).

The idea of 'gender bias' in the law and in legal education represents, of course, a fundamental challenge to the idea of justice as a woman blindfolded and weighing alternative arguments—the idea of justice as rational, objective and neutral. Instead, the idea of gender bias in the law and in legal education suggests that the interests of women are not equally valued by the law, and that women—as students, faculty members, and lawyers—do not have the same experiences and opportunities as men. While such contrasting visions of law and legal education have created some controversy both in Canada and elsewhere (Menkel-Meadow, 1988), the claims of gender bias also flow logically from the history of women as lawyers: their acceptance as lawyers only on condition that they accept the male standards of the law and the legal profession. In this way, the issues of gender bias in the law and in the legal profession in Canada in the 1980s represent a continuing legacy from the history of women as lawyers.

From the perspective of the history of women in the legal profession, and particularly from the perspective of the cases denying their admission as lawyers in Canada, the current challenge to the male standard is occurring in the context of the recent and dramatic increase in the numbers of women in the legal profession. So long as the numbers of women remained 'miniscule', it was possible to maintain the male standards embedded in law and legal education, and to permit women to participate as lawyers on the basis of their individual success in conforming to such standards. Like Portia in *The Merchant of Venice*, women were entitled to practise law so long as they appeared to be men; indeed, their success as lawyers may have depended on the extent to which they exhibited no outward signs of being women. With significantly increased numbers, however, the acceptance of maleness as *the* standard in the legal system appears increasingly inappropriate; when the profession includes ever larger numbers of women as well as men, the idea that Portia wants to win the case on her own terms and in her own identity seems hardly surprising. In this context, the current issues about gender bias in the law and in legal education represent a continuation of the challenges to law and to the legal profession initiated almost a century ago by Clara Brett Martin, Mabel Penury French and Annie Macdonald Langstaff.

Because the numbers revolution has been most dramatic in the law schools, moreover, it is not surprising that issues about gender bias —in particular, the prevalence of the male standard—have surfaced most frequently there in recent years. For some observers, the primary concern has been the content of legal education: the role of law in maintaining patriarchal relations between women and men and the pervasiveness of the male standard in legal concepts.

> Man has been and is the norm, not only in the minds of the
> seventeenth century grammarians who embedded he-n ss in language,
> but in notions of the rights of 'man', the nine 'man' bench, and the
> ubiquitous 'ordinary reasonable man' who is both the litmus of legal
> rationality and the constituent base of 'community standards' . . . Law
> is a vital instrument in the hegemony of male supremacy, for it
> legitimates the patriarchal form of family, male control of women's
> bodies and the separation of public and private life (O'Brien and
> McIntyre, 1986: 84–5).

For others, the primary focus has been on the teaching process itself, including the 'hidden curriculum', the classroom behaviour of both teachers and students, and the effect of legal education experiences on women and men who will become members of the legal profession in the future:

> The value messages in the 'hidden curriculum' of legal education relate
> to two separate but overlapping issues. The first is whether there is
> equality in education. Does our behaviour as teachers convey, whether
> we mean it or not, a lack of commitment to the value of sexual

equality? Does our behaviour convey the message to women 'you are not equal'? Secondly, there is the question of education for equality. Are we teaching, in a normative sense, that women ought not to be treated as equals? . . . Lawyers who do not comprehend the ways in which women are oppressed in our society will hardly be able to represent women clients effectively (Boyle, 1986: 102).

These kinds of questions about values embedded in principles of law and in the methods of legal education have also resulted in preliminary efforts to document the experiences of women and men law students and the content of their legal education experiences. At Toronto's Osgoode Hall Law School, for example, a group of students designed and implemented a project in 1987 to identify attitudes of faculty and students about gender and its impact on classroom dynamics. The study was inspired by and based to some extent on research undertaken at Harvard and reported in 1985 (Krupnick, 1985). Similar concerns about classroom activities and their differential impact on women and men students were expressed in a document entitled 'Women's Silence in the Classroom' submitted to the Faculty of Law at Yale University in 1986–87 (Weiss and Melling, 1988).

The Osgoode Hall project included observations of first year classes over a period of about two-and-a-half weeks, and questionnaires to faculty members teaching the same first year classes. The classroom observations included identifying the sex of every speaker (both faculty members and students) in each class during the regular teaching period, and the length of time during which professors and students spoke during each teaching period. The classroom observations also identified how teacher/student interaction was initiated: whether the professor acknowledged the student's hand; whether a student spontaneously interjected in the midst of an ongoing dialogue; or whether the professor addressed or questioned a student who had not raised his or her hand (a 'cold-call') (Attridge and Bunting et al., 1987: 8).

The results of the project offered some interesting data about the dynamics of law school classrooms. The project found that professors, both male and female, spoke for about 90 per cent of class time, with male professors speaking only slightly more of the time than their female colleagues. However, the comparisons of male and female students, represented in all these classes in approximately equal numbers, were more dramatic:

Male students participate[d] for periods of time three times longer than female students, and even more so in female professors' classes. This reflect[ed] at least a higher frequency of opportunity, if not length per interaction as well: men put up their hands two times more often, [were] recognised two times as often, [kept] their hands up while others [were] speaking, and [spoke] more often before being recognised by the professor. Female students raise[d] their hands more often and [were] recognised at a slightly higher rate in female professors' classes (Attridge and Bunting et al., 1987: 14–15).

The questionnaire to professors also produced some interesting results. In response to a question about the relative importance of a number of factors in the selection of course materials, the most significant factors identified by respondents were 'policy', 'continuity between sections' and 'ready availability'. However, 'male professors considere[d] gender balance to be less important, and authoritativeness significantly more important' by comparison with their female colleagues. Female professors said they were 'familiar' with feminist authors and literature, while male professors responded that they were only 'somewhat familiar'. And although female professors assigned extra class readings as often as their male colleagues, they reported that they assigned feminist readings 'approximately once per month' by comparison with 'once per semester' for male professors (Attridge and Bunting et al., 1987: 17).

Not surprisingly, the students involved in the project recommended the need for changes in the classroom experience and the dynamics of interaction for men and women law students. At the same time, however, they recognised a need for simultaneous changes in the fundamental structures of law (Attridge and Bunting et al., 1987: 33; Rifkin, 1980) and of legal education (Attridge and Bunting et al., 1987: 32–5; Pickard, 1986: 152) as the basis for achieving equality for men and women law students.[8]

Yet, while the rationale for rethinking the male standards of law and legal education has become increasingly clear, the process of achieving such changes remains less obvious. To the extent that existing male standards appear to present structural barriers, some commentators have suggested the need for systemic rather than individualistic solutions (Moss Kanter, 1977; Fuchs Epstein, 1981). These would include recruitment of women law teachers in significant numbers, systematic reviews of course content and approaches to teaching, seminars for law teachers about how to encourage effectively those students who are currently marginalised in law schools, and the creation of flexible institutional structures for responding to gender bias and other similar concerns (Boyle, 1986; Moss Kanter, 1978; Menkel-Meadow, 1987).

Systemic changes may also be controversial, however. As Boyle has noted, there are consequences for those who raise such issues:

I think more than twice about raising feminist values in a classroom when there is a danger that I will be accused of incompetence, have my class disrupted by people to whom freedom of speech means their freedom to attack me through pornography, and have to work in a setting in which I cannot post a notice without it being ripped down or defaced (Boyle, 1986: 111).

A student project at Queen's University also demonstrated the difficulties experienced by individuals, and by the institution as a whole, as a result of efforts to reveal gender bias in the educational setting. Out of 228 responses to a questionnaire distributed to all students, 61 per cent responded that they had encountered/witnessed sexism at the law school; 72 per cent of female respondents and 53 per cent of male respondents reported in this way. The written comments on some questionnaires demonstrated the tension surrounding efforts to change the curriculum and existing approaches to teaching in order to eliminate gender bias: as one student stated:

> I would like to learn the law; nothing more . . . I want to work within the male system. I don't want to be associated with a law school that is considered feminist and less worthy by the male system . . . (Cohen and Reddon, 1988: 12).

Just as societal ideas about the appropriateness of women becoming lawyers created controversy at the turn of the century, however, so the means of 'transforming' existing male standards in law within the legal profession and in the law schools is not without controversy. Indeed, as one writer has suggested, 'legal education may never be the same' (Menkel-Meadow: 1988).

'TRANSFORMING' LAW AND LAWYERING

The process of 'transformation' of societal ideas, particularly about appropriate roles for women and men, is a dynamic one, shifting constantly according to particular events and ideas. The history of the first women lawyers in Canada offers some useful insights about the ways in which changes in legal ideas occurred at the turn of the century,[9] insights which may be of assistance as the legal profession searches for more appropriate measures to respond to its 'revolution in numbers' at the end of the twentieth century. In the first place, the achievement of roles for women as lawyers occurred only after the same arguments about their suitability for the profession had been made in a number of different provinces, both in courts and in the legislatures. This observation suggests that the making of sex equality arguments, for women lawyers as for other women, requires some degree of general societal familiarity before the arguments will be broadly accepted and reflected in judges' decisions.

Second, for all three of the women who asserted claims to be admitted to the legal profession, the making of arguments favouring their admission, both in the courts and in the legislatures, was often done by allies, both men and women, who were in positions of some influence. This factor suggests the need to give some consideration to the persons who present sex equality arguments as well as the content of the arguments themselves. Perhaps more significantly, it also suggests a need for those in positions of influence (including senior partners in law firms, judges, law deans and professors—both women and men) to recognise their special responsibility for furthering sex equality claims in the law and within the profession.

The three litigated cases also demonstrate that women claimants were significantly more successful as a result of lobbying efforts in provincial legislatures than they were in courts, despite their absence at that time from the ranks of legislators, and even voters, as from the legal profession itself. In the early cases, all of the judges except Mr Justice Lavergne in *Langstaff* accepted a narrowly-defined 'interpretative' role for the court rather than a more creative one even though there were no binding legal precedents. While some commentators have suggested that the enactment of the Canadian Charter of Rights and Freedoms may have transformed the role of courts in Canada to one that is more involved with lawmaking, particularly in matters of equality (Bayefsky and Eberts, 1987), the general issue of the role of courts in matters concerning equality for women in the legal profession is still largely unresolved.

Yet, it may be that there is a more significant connection between the early cases about women as lawyers and the current efforts to alter the male standard of law and lawyering within the law schools. If the litigation in the early cases can be perceived as efforts to focus the issues, to define the arguments, and to concretise societal concerns about appropriate sex roles at the turn of the century, the claimants' defeats in their court cases might be seen as catalysts in highlighting the issues publicly in specific and concrete situations, thereby providing the impetus for public pressure for legislative action. By seeing the litigation-legislative process as a continuum, rather than as two discrete activities operating quite separately from one another, court cases can be recognised as a significant part of the challenge to contemporary societal ideas about appropriate roles for men and women.

In this way, the cases about the admission of women as lawyers have ongoing relevance to women lawyers in the 1980s and 1990s in their efforts to challenge the maleness of law and the process of lawyering. They can be seen as an integral part of the continuum of women's challenge to male exclusivity in the law and in the legal profession in the twentieth century. Seen this way, the history of Clara Brett Martin, Mabel Penury French and Annie Macdonald Langstaff is a part of the history of all women who are lawyers in the 1980s and 1990s, whether they choose to accept the existing male standard or to challenge it.[10] And for the legal profession in Canada, the ideas debated at the turn of the century in the cases concerning the admission of women as lawyers offer critical insights about the nature of the 'revolution' now occurring from within:

> We are living in an age of unprecedented transformation. We are in the process of becoming . . . Women at long last are demanding, as men did in the Renaissance, the right to explain, the right to define . . . (Lerner, 1986: 229).

Moreover, the challenge presented by women lawyers in the 1980s and 1990s represents only the beginning of the transformation of law and the legal profession now underway. Just as women were once excluded from the profession, so were other 'outsiders' unprotected by laws and prevented from joining the profession. And just as women were admitted to the profession on the basis of their conformity to an existing male standard, so other 'outsiders' have been admitted on such terms. On this basis, the challenges to redefine law in women's interests and to redefine appropriate roles for women and men as lawyers are just part of a larger process to make the law more responsive to all members of society, and to make the legal profession accept and value equally the talents and experiences of all women and men in a modern multicultural community:

> Feminist insights into the power of unstated norms demand just this perpetual reconsideration of the point of view buried within social arrangements and in critiques of them, the point of view that makes some differences matter and others irrelevant. Otherwise, outsiders who become insiders simply define new groups as 'other' . . . The concerted and persistent search for excluded points of view and the acceptance of their challenges are equally critical to feminist theory and practice . . . (Minow, 1988: 60).

In this context, a vision of justice in which Portia has a recognised identity as a woman in our legal system and in the law schools is only the beginning. Such a vision of justice surely requires us to ensure equal justice for Shylock too, as for all those 'others' who have been 'outsiders' in our legal system.

The research assistance of Shelagh O'Connell and Heather Ritchie, both of the Class of 1989 at Osgoode Hall Law School, is gratefully acknowledged; as is the technical assistance of Hazel Pollack; the warm support of Reg Graycar, Jenny Morgan and Margaret Thornton; and the enthusiasm and ideas of my students and especially of my colleague Diana Majury in my course in Law, Gender, Equality.

I am also most grateful to colleagues at the Law and Gender conference in Sydney in December 1987 for comments and suggestions about women lawyers and the relationship of history to current issues about women in the legal profession; and to both York University and Osgoode Hall Law School for travel assistance to attend the Law and Gender conference in Australia.

7

Affirmative action and legal knowledge: planting seeds in plowed-up ground

As twentieth-century scholars, we are pursued by the relativity of knowledge. Anthropologists, historians of science, feminist theorists, and critical legal scholars are among those attempting to understand the degree to which knowledge is contingent or autonomous, real or imagined, accidental or purposeful (Minow, 1987). Those outside the traditional centre of academia intuit that their personal knowledge—what they hold true and dear, what is real to them—often comes from their life experience as outsiders (Diamond and Edwards, 1977).[1] Women report the experience of a different reality, a different morality.[2] People of colour find an affinity of knowledge in their separate caucuses that they do not find in predominantly white settings. Knowledge at the academic centre, however, stands monumental and unchanged by the separate knowledges that groups of outsiders are nurturing at the academic margins.

Affirmative action, a concept we have accepted in terms of bringing new colours and shapes of human bodies into the law schools, should also apply to our primary function as scholars: the exploration of human knowledge. The new individuals we are bringing to the law schools also bring new ideas about law. Instead of bending their minds to conform to the knowledge of the formerly segregated law school, perhaps we should bend our shared legal knowledge to accommodate new visions.

This chapter was originally published in a slightly different form in (1988) 11 *Harvard Women's Law Journal* 1.

*OLD GARDENS: THE LANDSCAPE OF SEGREGATED LEGAL
KNOWLEDGE*

This proposal suggests specific action to end apartheid in legal knowledge. Apartheid is evident in the books shelved, in the journals read, and in the sources considered in the process of legal scholarship. Recurring citations in prestigious legal writing, particularly in theoretical writing, are largely segregated, as Richard Delgado noted in his article, 'The Imperial Scholar' (Delgado, 1984). This segregation results in a legal knowledge uninformed by the rich and provocative knowledge of outsiders.

One can discern the landscape of segregated legal knowledge by reading the law reviews of elite law schools. Certain citations appear with such frequency that they have become *de rigueur* for anyone wishing to engage in discourse within that particular academic realm (Kuhn, 1970). While women authors are, commendably, increasingly represented in the articles and citations, an informal review indicates that they are cited with far less regularity than men. People of colour fare even less well than women in citation counts, following the familiar pattern of affirmative action in admissions and employment: white women are integrated first, and in limited numbers, followed by men of colour, then women of colour, each at dramatically decreasing rates (Chused, 1985: 572; Lawrence, 1986).

Citation counts are a standard measure of academic prestige (Fiedler and Hart, 1986). Scholars proceed in research and information-gathering by following a trail of footnotes. In addition to following footnotes, people cite what they have read and discussed with their academic friends. When their reading and their circle of friends are limited, their citations become limited. The citations then breed further self-reference. This process ignores a basic fact of human psychology: human beings learn and grow through interaction with difference, not by reproducing what they already know (Miller, 1976). A system of legal education that ignores the outsiders' perspectives artificially restricts and stultifies the scholarly imagination (Kitano, 1980). Segregated scholarship also conveys the implicit message of the inferiority of the excluded scholarship. Like segregation in housing, schooling, and private clubs, segregation in citations denies the worth of the excluded groups.

When outsiders' perspectives are ignored in legal scholarship, not only do we lose important ideas and insights, but we also fail in our most traditional role as educators. We fail to prepare future practitioners for effective advocacy and policy formation in a world populated by women and men of differing points of view. We also fail in traditional affirmative action goals (McMillen, 1987). Recruitment and retention of women and people of colour in faculty positions, for example, are exceedingly difficult when such candidates perceive the law schools as hostile worlds of tilted knowledge, and where their scholarship fails to claim the attention of dominant legal academicians (Austin, 1986).

PLOWING UP THE GROUND: ALTERING THE LANDSCAPE OF LIMITED LEGAL KNOWLEDGE

'Those who profess to favor freedom and yet deprecate agitation . . . want crops without plowing up the ground, they want rain without thunder and lightning. They want the ocean without the roar of its many voices' (Martin, 1984). A theory of affirmative action scholarship is worthless without a practice. This section sets forth concrete steps for desegregation of legal knowledge.

Established scholars can start the process of eradicating apartheid in legal knowledge by making a deliberate effort to buy, order, read, cite, discuss, and teach outsiders' scholarship. When buying twenty books in a newly-discovered bookstore, for example, the affirmative action scholar should ascertain that some of them are written by white women, women of colour, and men of colour.[3] If none are available, a formal inquiry is appropriate. The scholar can put pressure on the bookselling and publishing industries to supply outsiders' scholarship. Quotas will help the particularly recalcitrant buyer, and are suggested here in the literal sense. Examples include: 1. *Numerical Goals:* I will buy five books by women of colour this year. 2. *Alternative Selection:* For every book I buy authored by a man, I will buy one authored by a woman. 3. *Moratoriums:* I will not buy any mainstream books this summer until I make corrections in my deficient knowledge of outsider scholarship.[4]

Similarly, the affirmative action scholar will ensure that some of the materials, in a stack of books and articles set aside for weekend reading, are authored by outsiders. When writing an article or book, the newly conscious scholar might consider ways in which outsider scholarship could enhance the piece. Once one begins a formal reading programme in outsider scholarship, the citation goal is easily met. As scholars, we are inspired by what we read, and the affirmative action reader will delight in the new insights gleaned from writers previously unknown. Citing outsider scholarship is a political act. Tenure and promotion-review committees typically ask whether a candidate's work is cited. Readers look to citations to determine whether an article speaks to them. When Martha Minow, a Harvard law school professor, cites Audre Lorde, she is saying to women, to people of colour, and to lesbians, 'I am talking to you. I am learning from you' (Minow, 1987). This act brings outsiders into the world of Harvardian discourse, and encourages them to continue writing. It challenges other readers to expand their sources, and prevents the ghettoisation of outsider writing.

Scholars can also engage in affirmative action when making out cheques for dues and subscriptions by searching out fora that attract outsiders' work, and by learning to read documentary sources other than law review articles. Some of the best theoretical statements are found in position papers, briefs, speeches, op-ed pieces and other non-academic publications (Aptheker, 1965). Outsiders' scholarship is often front-line scholarship. The luxury of law review writing is not always available to scholars whose legal and theoretical skills are called first to battle against racism and sexism. If originality, exhaustive research, theory-building, conceptualisation, doctrinal facility, and historical perspective are the measures of quality legal scholarship, then briefs in test-case litigation qualify as scholarship.[5] To the extent that briefs frame cases and cases become raw material for casebooks and law review articles, many writers are inadvertently failing to attribute the proper origin of innovations in legal concepts and changes in the law.

In addition to enlarging the scope of what one reads, cites and teaches to include the works of outsiders, scholars and others in the legal profession can promote affirmative action goals as organisers of meetings, panel discussions, and symposia. Inviting an outsider to present a paper, particularly if publication is likely to result, is an empowering gesture that will result in a better session for all participants.[6] Those privileged by frequent invitations to participate in such events might develop the habit of asking whether members of underrepresented groups will also receive invitations and encourage strategies for assuring outsider attendance. Those attending academic meetings can call attention to absences that reveal ideology by questioning the intellectual legitimacy of a panel discussion devoid of a female voice, or of a conference unattended by people of colour.

Editors, librarians, book reviewers, and publishers can also participate in affirmative action scholarship, and consumers of their services can request that they do so. Law review editors, for example, should take special care to invite outsider scholars to contribute, and book reviewers should analyse, criticise, and bring to the fore deserving outsider works.

Law students, as well, can exercise affirmative action scholarship. Students are perhaps unaware of the power they hold as the fee-paying consumers of legal education. Students can inquire of professors and administrators whether outsider scholarship was considered in the compilation of required readings. They can conduct surveys, perhaps as an independent study project, exploring the degree of segregated knowledge in the law schools. Empirical study of the assigned readings in the first year curriculum, for example, might reveal a degree of segregation previously unnoticed by the faculty. Students can organise fora to bring outsider voices to law schools, and they can take responsibility for their own education, seeking out and studying the materials law schools fail to hand to them. The habit of complicity, of accepting without challenge what one is provided by established power, is dangerous and anti-democratic. Law schools are relatively safe places to risk conflict and to develop the habit of self-education (Worden, 1986).

Finally, affirmative action in legal scholarship requires new skills of listening. The voices bringing new knowledge are sometimes faint and self-effacing, at other times brash and discordant. To the extent that our past complicity in academic segregation has contributed to these different tones, we should strive to understand their origin and listen carefully for the truth they may hide. Professor Harry Kitano suggests that minority group writers having suffered under racist conditions, 'are likely to write with great emotion and little patience' (Kitano, 1980: 8).

Implicit in this proposal is the belief that intellectual inquiry is a valid adjunct to movements for positive social change. I do not suggest that scholars are the vanguard of such change. They are not. The creation and dissemination of collective knowledge is, however, an important element of social transformation. Scholars must continue to do what they do best in a way that will promote an end to all forms of oppression. Only a privileged minority of world citizens receive a university education. Exercising that privilege without thought to inclusion of outsiders supports the continuation of an exclusionary system, and deprives all scholars of the full breadth of intellectual stimulation and rigour we require.

NEW GARDENS: THE LANDSCAPE OF INTEGRATED LEGAL KNOWLEDGE

It is difficult to imagine a landscape of integrated legal knowledge, for we have never brought together all the hands we need to create that landscape. Feminist theory tells us that the outsider's voice is likely to change the way we understand the world. We do not yet know whether the difference women bring is simply a temporal reaction to patriarchy or whether it is, as some hope, a revolutionary difference that will remake law to bring about a more humane world (MacKinnon, 1985a).[7] We will not know what we can learn until we use affirmative action in scholarship to welcome newcomers to the legal profession.

The new voices will emphasise difference. Confronting difference will give new vigour to theoretical debate. The outsider's different knowledge of discrimination, for example, is concrete and personal.[8] To the extent legal discourse is distillable into conflicts over the distribution of resources, the voice of the poor will force us to discuss such conflicts with full awareness of the reality of poverty. Standard jurisprudential discourse, with its tendency to abstraction, will be forced to confront the harsh edge of realism. True affirmative action in law schools requires that the perspective of outsiders is considered as a matter of course in all discussions of doctrine and policy, and is expressed freely without fear of being labelled irrelevant or unrealistic. An affirmative action law school would respect those views by including them in readings, citations, symposia, library acquisitions, conferences, and classroom discussion. When we do this, we will live and work a different kind of academic life, one more invigorating and surprising than that we live now.

WEEDS: OBJECTIONS TO AFFIRMATIVE ACTION IN LEGAL SCHOLARSHIP

In the spirit of the new legal scholarship that allows for self-doubt (Gordon, 1984), this section considers troublesome objections to the concept of affirmative action scholarship.

First, an attempt to seek out and use outsider scholarship can appear patronising and can reveal to others an embarrassing lack of knowledge. Do we grant unwelcome privilege to outsiders by seeking out their work, exercising an infatuation with difference that serves only to reinforce existing concepts of otherness? Do we maintain a hierarchical relationship of patron and token outsider by choosing whom to include?

The danger of missing out altogether on an important body of knowledge seems, on balance, a greater risk. The writers of the Harlem renaissance struggled with the conflicting need for and desire to reject white patronage. For example, as offensive as white preference for 'dialect' poetry was, the Harlem writers continued to seek publication in white-dominated presses (Hull, 1984; Rampersad, 1986). The white patronage they exacted helped develop and preserve an American art and literature integral to our cultural history. My conclusion from this historical incident is that the risk of offensive patronage and inevitable cross-cultural misunderstanding was worth the benefit to both Black culture and mainstream American culture that is the legacy of the Harlem renaissance.

Thinking people can avoid the grossest offences by creating fora for discussion of the patronage dilemma and by learning a new academic etiquette. We might stop saying 'American' or 'Australian' when we mean 'white', or 'women' when we mean 'white women'.

We might learn the basic facts of the experience of outsider groups. We might learn why a *sansei* can't speak Japanese, what Black scholars are saying about capitalising 'Black,' and how many women in a class of 100 are probable victims of sex abuse. These are the things we learn from exposure to difference. We learn the facts and the code of behaviour that relieve us from constant reassessment of our ability to commune successfully with one another. Until we acquire these new skills—skills we have been deprived of by our own segregated backgrounds—we will wound and stumble and long for retreat into the familiar singularity of segregated life.

In addition to the discomfort arising from our lack of social skill at integrated life, there is the dual danger of overrating or underrating outsider work. Insiders may feel they are not free to criticise outsider scholarship. I have noticed in myself, for example, an immediate reaction of rage when someone tells me they did not like *The Civil Rights Chronicles* (Bell, 1985). Where does this rage come from? Does it mean that I presume anyone who does not have a near-religious experience upon reading Derrick Bell is a racist? This would be an unfair assumption, and an overprotective attitude toward Professor Bell, whose stature as a scholar can and will receive public criticism. While 'not bad, considering' and 'bad, such a pity' comments can drip with racism and sexism, fair public and private criticism is valuable to all scholars. In the legal profession, recognition is gained as often by critique as by praise. Witness the citation frequency and concomitant must-read status accorded to Rawls and Dworkin in critical legal studies literature, or of Duncan Kennedy in the writings of the Right. Fair criticism is thus consistent with affirmative action goals. Intellectual criticism directed against vulnerable, isolated, untenured, and disempowered scholars, however, carries different political implications than criticism of outsider scholars surrounded by a critical mass of other empowered outsiders. Fair criticism requires the reader to understand a particular genre before criticising, and to strive for freedom from race/class/gender/culture bias.[9] It requires as well an active commitment to numerical affirmative-action hiring.

Exposure will chip away at the walls between us, and academic insiders and outsiders will benefit from scholarly exchange across those crumbling walls. The more outsider scholarship critics read, the more informed their criticism will be. Scholarship arises in a context. Just as the full impact of James Joyce or Igor Stravinsky becomes clear only after understanding the state of the art they responded to, so does the full sweep of *The Civil Rights Chronicles* become evident only within the context of Afro-American history, Afro-American rhetorical style, and Bell's previous work.

Concern about overburdening or imposing upon outsider scholars might also arise in acting upon this proposal for affirmative action scholarship. Given low numbers of outsider scholars, is it fair to ask them repeatedly to participate in symposia, to criticise drafts, or to review books? Perhaps it is best to leave them alone to write their tenure pieces. This concern carries two false assumptions. First is the assumption that there are only a handful of outsider scholars to share the burdens of presenting alternative perspectives. While there are fewer than one would hope, there are increasing numbers of white women and people of colour in law teaching, particularly in the United States. Active inclusion of these scholars will help end the myth, particularly prevalent at elite law schools, that outsider law professors are as rare as California condors.

The second false assumption is that active participation in the scholarly community will overburden outsider scholars and prevent them from doing their own important work. The opposite may well be true. Scholars attempting to produce articles alone in the law library sometimes fail because of the very isolation that is intended to promote writing. Writing is communicating, and it comes with natural ease and enthusiasm when the will to tell is strong. The will to tell, the will to teach, is roused when the scholar is actively, even angrily, engaged in discourse with other scholars. Thus, the rounds of symposia, retreats, and public speaking—and the concomitant feeling that others care about one's point of view—are significant precursors to good scholarship.

Another barrier to affirmative action in scholarship, sometimes called the collegiality problem, is the conflict, pain, and embarrassment that accompanies the introduction of difference. While we can strive to soften the edges of this conflict, we cannot avoid it, for the very goal of affirmative action is to change the way things are. Outsiders will expose and become targets for racism, sexism, and other 'isms' that are more easily buried when we pretend that law school revolves around narrowly-defined discourse. Outsiders will feel the characteristic frustration that arises when one is asked to educate others about what the others should already know. Conversely, white men will experience the terror of otherness when new voices arrive at law schools. No longer the referent of everyone else's difference, they may feel vulnerable and marginalised as outsiders grow in power; they may perceive themselves as objects of outsiders' bitter fantasies of revenge. Audre Lorde once said in response to a white woman's guilt and confusion in the face of Black anger: 'I do not exist to feel her pain for her' (Lorde, 1984). While I strive to understand and respect her statement, I do think we all must accept some responsibility for the pain we generate when we shake ourselves out of the casual racism and sexism that pervades our institutional homes.

We must also consider the dangers of complacency, assimilation and homogenisation. Once we have incorporated all voices, we may still remain keepers of law schools full of smart people talking to each other, divorced from the real world of struggle. Academe may prove a mellow monster amiably capable of drawing angry outsiders into its maw, where they will rest quietly, no longer a threat to existing power. I don't think this will happen. Assimilation is not possible in a world that is, unfortunately, still poisoned by resilient racism, sexism, class bias, and homophobia. Outsiders are all too frequently reminded of their difference. They are likely to remain aware and active qua outsiders until Frederick Douglass's dreamed of millenium—the time of true equality that is the reward for constant struggle.

The dangers of intellectual appropriation, imperialism, and colonisation also deserve attention. If mainstream scholars take the admonition to read and cite outsiders in their own work seriously, will they thereby enhance their own academic prestige by playing the new music to the old audience? Scholarship, to an extent, is appropriation with attribution. The danger of intrusion and preemption of outsider prerogatives necessitates an examination of the possibility of exploitation. Is it exploitative, for example, for an Asian-American to rely heavily on Black sources or for a white scholar to build an academic reputation writing about indigenous peoples? My answer thus far is that the telling of the story is important, and the voice-once-removed is sometimes the only one available to tell that story in the universities. In using the experience of another, careful attribution, acknowledgment, and disclaimer are appropriate, as well as an active commitment to bringing the outsiders themselves into the academic circle and to sharing any benefits accruing from publication.

Finally, any proposal for affirmative action scholarship will draw resistance from those who rightfully treasure academic freedom and who fear tyranny of any kind, including the tyranny of outsider pain. Thus it is necessary to clarify this proposal. The project proposed here is not one of establishing hierarchies of pain, or superiorities of difference. Rather it is one of recognising difference and thereby advancing our goals as scholars and political beings. Outsiders might want to discuss among themselves whether there is such a thing as reverse elitism, and learn to recognise when their frustration at insiders' inability to empathise is itself a conditioned response of the colonized, made irrespective of the merits of the insiders' efforts. As to insiders who feel coerced, no one is required to follow this proposal. The sceptical may wish to try it, with artificial enthusiasm, to see whether it works for them.

Like the city child planting a first garden, the sceptic may find something wonderful and obvious that was unknown before.

CASE STUDY: ONE TEACHER'S EXPERIENCE

On a recent visit to Australia, I reminded myself of affirmative action scholarship and sought out writing by Aboriginal people. The commercial and university bookstores had thin collections of materials pertaining to Aboriginal people, and had almost no works authored by Aboriginal people themselves. Complaints about this finally led me to Black Books, a small store operated at an Aboriginal college. Even at Black Books all the books on Aboriginal legal claims and land use, my research interests, were written by enlightened whites. The clerk, sensing my frustration, offered assistance, pointing out a section overflowing with poems and fiction by Black Australian writers. These works contained what I was looking for: insight into the jurisprudence of Aboriginal people—their ideas about land, about law, about government, about justice. Later, I realised, the best sources I have found for an indigenous voice are poems. Poets can self-proclaim their status as writers. Academic writers cannot. Semantically we differentiate between writers (unpublished) and authors (published), but a poet is a poet, regardless of commercial or state-defined status. Aboriginal writers, coming from a rich oral tradition and finding themselves excluded from academic writing, have become powerful poets and fiction-writers (see, for example Davis, 1983; Johnson, 1986; Walker, 1970; Weller, 1986).

This and other efforts to find and read outsider work led naturally to using this work in the classroom. In my American Legal History class, I have used excerpts from a book discovered through a self-imposed bookstore quota rule. The book is *Selma, Lord, Selma*, an oral history of two Black women who were children during the voter registration struggle in Selma, Alabama (Webb and Nelson, 1980). I use this excerpt in class first to describe the civil rights movement to students who have no personal recollection of it, and secondly to provoke a discussion on the power of rights rhetoric versus the limits of liberal legalism. Students in each of three classes have shed real tears over this story of two children who decided on their own, and without parental approval, to join the life-threatening confrontation at Edmund Pettus Bridge in order to win the right to vote for Blacks. This personalised account forces students to confront the power of legal ideals in a concrete way, and provides a useful counterpoint to articles challenging the efficacy of law reform. I know of no comparable piece for making this point. It is no accident that it took the words of two Black women to evoke that response.

The only other time I have seen students cry in class was when I read an Alice Walker essay on death and dying in contemporary America to illustrate a point in a torts class (Walker, 1985). The topic for the class was the underlying rationale for compensating wrongful death. The class was asked whether the rationale relates to an emerging human rights standard of dignified death. The Walker essay describes the death of an elderly Black woman who has lived a life full of work, friendship, gardens, and grandchildren. Her friends and family gather around her as she dies quietly in her home. Walker's female understanding of what she calls an 'excellent death' is a good foil for the standard analysis of wrongful death as compensation for economic loss to the survivors. Her reverence for death from old age provides a Black perspective as well: death from old age comes less often to the Black community, where police violence, sub-standard health care, crime, industrial accidents, and the ravages of poverty take disproportionate numbers of young lives—young lives devalued by the standard lost-future-earnings measure of damages. The broader perspective of torts issues that this article provided was a useful supplement to the casebook.

In addition to classroom material, affirmative action scholarship has helped me to think about law, justice, knowledge, and history in ways that have excited me and fuelled the desire to write. It has led me to new environments where I was welcomed with open arms, to others where I was told angrily, 'go study your own acts of oppression, leave us alone'. That anger never fails to wound; it is so familiar, and yet, I am told, not mine to know or understand. That anger first brings terror; it may be true, after all, that each of us is ultimately and coldly alone in this life. Subsequently, however, it brings resolve to learn more and to work harder to defeat the terror. The voices of outsiders, including the angry voices, speak with an urgency that pushes my pen and makes me a scholar, indebted to my sisters and brothers for what they have taught me.

In summary, for one law teacher, affirmative action in the pursuit of knowledge has quickened the chase, has worked in the classroom, and has brought forth this essay proposal. We are intellectual workers.[10] Our shared words can end apartheid on our bookshelves, and help to banish it from our lives.

A gardening handbook warns us to remove the seed heads of phlox every spring and plant anew the hybrid seed. Left alone to reseed, the phlox will soon revert to the old muddy-purple, disappointing the gardener who first planted a rainbow of lemon, white, garnet, lavender, and apricot. We must tend our garden lovingly, lest we revert to the boring world of one colour, one idea. Would that only aesthetics were at stake. Law, unfortunately, mediates much more. We are a people striving for peace and economic security in a world that possesses neither. We cannot afford to exclude the strengths of any of us in the difficult days ahead.

Endnotes

Ch 2

1   For further discussion of the significance for feminism of this 'reconsideration' of biology and the sexed body, see (1987) 5 *Australian Feminist Studies*—special issue on *Feminism and the Body*.

2   For a historical discussion of the resonances of the encounter between masculinism and feminism, see Lake, 1986; Allen, 1987b.

Ch 3

1   For more reserved conclusions from more ambiguous research findings on the net-widening effects of diversionary policies in Great Britain, see Bottomley and Pease (1986: 118–27).

2   American research has also assessed in-service programmes in juvenile community-based corrections as failures (Shorts, 1986).

3   See Charlotte Mitra's insightful analysis of masculinist judges' trivialisation of the harm caused to young girls by father–daughter rape (Mitra, 1987).

Ch 4

1   For constitutional reasons, the Family Law Act, a federal law, was previously applicable only to 'children of a marriage' (see Jessep and Chisholm, 1985; Guthrie and Kingshott, 1987). However, this situation changed after significant amendments to the Family Law Act which came into force from April 1988.

2   For a more detailed discussion of the Child Support Scheme, see Graycar, 1989a.

3   Senator Susan Ryan was, until January 1988, the federal government Minister responsible for Women's Affairs.

4   For further elaboration of some of these themes, see Graycar, 1989b.

5   Significantly, men were far more likely to have repartnered than women at the time of interview (McDonald, 1986: 58–9). It should also be noted, however, that an important question, namely, equal sharing of what, is often left out of the matrimonial property debate. This is because various

forms of property, such as business assets and future interests in superannuation are rarely put into the 'pool' for distribution.

Ch 6

1   A legislative amendment in 1892 permitted women to be admitted to law practice as solicitors and another in 1895 permitted them to practise as barristers-at-law. For an account of the efforts to achieve these legislative changes, see Backhouse, 1985; and Riddell, 1918.

2   In his judgment, Mr Justice Barker relied greatly on the decision of Mr Justice Bradley in *Bradwell v Illinois* (1837 United States Supreme Court). In that decision, Mr Justice Bradley adopted the idea of 'separate spheres' for men and women, and his views were quoted extensively by Mr Justice Barker in *In re French*:

> ... the civil law, as well as nature herself, has always recognized a wide difference in the respective spheres and destinies of man and woman. Man is, or should be, woman's protector and defender. The natural and proper timidity and delicacy which belongs to the female sex evidently unfits it for many of the occupations of civil life. The constitution of the family organization, which is founded in the divine ordinance as well as in the nature of things, indicates the domestic sphere as that which properly belongs to the domain and functions of womanhood ... (*In re French*, 1906: 365).

3   A writ of mandamus is a court order directed to an administrative body or official commanding the performance of a particular act, as specified in the order, and within the public duty of the administrative body or official.

4   In Canada, the issue of whether women were 'persons' under the law was not finally determined until the 'Person's' case, *Edwards v Attorney General for Canada* (1930). Ironically, it was the decision of the Judicial Committee of the Privy Council which confirmed women's legal personhood in a successful appeal from a negative conclusion on the part of the Supreme Court of Canada (Mossman, 1986, 1987). For a scathing analysis of the Privy Council decision, however, see Henderson, 1929:

> ... it must seem evident to one who carefully considers the judgment that it is not written in strict accordance with well understood legal principles, and can be explained only by bearing in mind the proposition firstly outlined that there is the outstanding difference between the Supreme Court of Canada and the Privy Council that the one is a Court of law, subject to all the restrictions of a Court of law, and that the other has no limitations at all, is not bound to follow precedent nor to determine matters upon grounds of law alone but is entitled, if not obliged, to advise his Majesty on grounds of public policy and to take into account matters of political expediency ... (Henderson, 1929: 628).

5   In New Brunswick and in British Columbia, the legislation was called

An Act to Remove the Disability of Women so far as relates to the Study and Practice of the Law. In New Brunswick, for example, section 1 of the statute enacted in 1906 provided as follows:

> Notwithstanding any law, regulation, by-law or custom to the contrary, women shall be admitted to the study of the law, and shall be called and admitted as barristers and attorneys, *upon the same terms, and subject to the like conditions and regulations as men* [my emphasis].

6   Abel is referring to the demographic changes in the United States, but has elsewhere suggested that the changes occurring in the United States were replicated in other western nations, including Canada and Australia (Abel, 1985).

7   This article focused on the impact on law schools of the reports of a number of American task forces on the status of women in the courts. The first state Supreme Court Task Force in New Jersey was established in 1982. New York issued its report in 1986 and Rhode Island in 1987. Task force reports are underway in Colorado, Connecticut, Massachusetts, California, Michigan, Minnesota, Florida, Illinois, Washington, Arizona, Utah, Maryland, Nevada and Hawaii (Schneider, 1988: 87).

In addition, the American Bar Association's Task Force on Women in the Legal Profession recently recommended a number of measures to improve the opportunities for women to participate effectively as members of the legal profession. The ABA Task Force Report reiterated the need to look beyond the numbers of women in the profession:

> While several witnesses emphasized the great strides women have made in entering and succeeding in the profession, most participants at the hearings expressed frustration and disillusionment that barriers are still great and that progress had been far slower than expected. Witnesses cautioned that we must not be lulled into complacency about the status of women in the profession simply because the numbers of women entering the profession continue to increase (ABA, Summary of Hearings, 1988: 2).

The Canadian Bar Association passed a resolution in August 1988 calling upon the federal government to establish a Tak Force on Gender Equality to:

(1)   investigate whether or what gender discrimination exists in the Canadian legal system; and
(2)   make recommendations to eliminate gender discrimination in the Canadian legal system (CBA Resolution #3, August 1988).

The creation of a National Task Force on Gender Equality in the Courts was also recommended by the Report of the Manitoba Association of Women and the Law, *Gender Equality in the Courts* (November 1988). The Report canvassed 'the issue of gender unfairness in the Canadian legal system through case analysis of selected Manitoba decisions in the areas of family law and personal injury awards and through a review of the treatment of female lawyers, law students, law faculty, witnesses and court personnel by the Canadian legal system' (Report, at 1).

8   For older studies about sex differences among law students, see Robert and Winter, 1978; and Rathjen, 1976. More recently, a pilot study in the United States on gender bias in law school classrooms concluded that:

> Despite the increasing number of women entering law school, men still view women, consciously or unconsciously, as abnormal, as strangers or outsiders. Women, because of gender, are not naturally menbers of the 'club'. Thus the club members expect women to change and adapt—to become more like men—in order to join the club. Few question the extent to which becoming more like men accomplishes the stated goal of the club—the training of people who will see to the fair and impartial development, interpretation, and administration of the law (Lovell Banks, 1988).

The Lovell Banks study was based on a questionnaire originally developed by Hall and Sandler, 1982. See also Morgan, 1989.

9   Carol Smart's analysis of the 'uneven development' of the law, which 'recognises the distinctions between law-as-legislation and the effects of law, or law-in-practice,' is a helpful way of thinking about the law reform process in the context of feminist objectives and strategies (Smart, 1986: 117). In the context of this chapter, however, I am attempting to see the relationship between the conception of ideas about sex roles and the legal reform process. In this context, the idea of the law's uneven development is useful in trying to understand the complex process by which ideas become concretised for the purpose of political action as a result of the litigation/law reform process.

10   See, for example, *Mary Lou Fassel et al. v York University* (unreported), a complaint to the Ontario Human Rights Commission concerning sex discrimination at Osgoode Hall Law School in 1987.

[Editor's note: This involved over 100 lawyers, academics and law students who filed a complaint with the Ontario Human Rights Commission concerning the failure of York University and Osgoode Hall Law School to appoint Mary Jane Mossman as dean of Osgoode Hall Law School in 1987, and the failure of the school and university to provide gender equality for women students.

The complaint sought remedies designed to redress what the complainants alleged was a longstanding practice of sex discrimination. At the time of publication, the complaint was tentatively settled through an agreement which, amongst other things, acknowledged gender equality as the priority issue at Osgoode Hall Law School; devoted substantial funding to the Clara Brett Martin Institute which is to undertake research in feminist legal scholarship and establishes a Mary Jane Mossman scholarship for graduate students undertaking research in feminist legal studies (see 'Women win pledge in law school row', *Toronto Globe and Mail*, 20 September 1989: A14; '$1 million pledge ends rights fight at law school', *Toronto Star*, 20 September 1989: A1).]

Ch 7

1 'Outsiders' is used throughout the remainder of this chapter to encompass various out-groups, including women, people of colour, poor and working people, gays and lesbians, indigenous people, and other subordinated groups who have suffered historical underrepresentation and silencing in the law schools. 'Outsiders' is an awkward term, used here experimentally to avoid the use of 'minority.' The outsiders collectively are a numerical majority, as Professor Haunani-Kay Trask has pointed out to me. The inclusive term is not intended to deny the need for separate consideration of the circumstances of each group. It is a semantic convenience used here to discuss the need for epistemological inclusion of the views of many dominated groups.

2 See eg, Gilligan, 1982. Gilligan's description of a separate female experience is discussed and critiqued in Dubois, Dunlap, Gilligan, MacKinnon and Menkel-Meadow, 1985 (hereafter 'Feminist Discourse'). For a discussion of the unique attributes of female perception and writing see Abel, 1982.

3 bell hooks reminds us that white women and women of colour are different in some ways, similar in others (hooks, 1981).

4 For a discussion of the moral and theoretical basis of affirmative action, see Edley, 1986.

5 Valuable examples of non-law review scholarship include Plaintiff's Petition for Writ of Error Corum Nobis and Memorandum of Points and Authorities, *Korematsu v. United States*, 584F. Supp. 1406 (N.D. Cal. 1984) (No. CR-27635W) (written by the predominantly Asian-American *Korematsu* Legal Team, arguing for reversal of the United States Supreme Court's decision allowing war-time internment of Japanese-Americans).

   The Amici Curiae Brief of the Feminist Anti-Censorship Taskforce, et al., *American Booksellers Ass'n Inc. v. Hudnut*, 771 F.2d 323 (7th Cir. 1985), is an excellent treatment by feminists of the first amendment/pornography dilemma: see FACT, 1987–8.

6 In this regard the author would like to thank the Harvard Women's Law Association and the Australian Law and Society Association for organising conferences on gender issues at which preliminary versions of this essay were presented.

7 Catharine MacKinnon argues that true women's morality is unknowable given the reality of patriarchal dominance. In her words, women are not free to articulate their own particularities while 'this foot [is] on our necks' (MacKinnon, 1985a: 28).

8 This point was made repeatedly in the comments on feminist jurisprudence published in the American Association of Law Schools Jurisprudence Section Newsletter, November 1987.

9 For an example of an informed critical response to Black nationalist poetry, see Jordan, 1986.

10 Anne Fagan Ginger, scholar, activist, and author, uses the term 'intellectual workers' in urging law students to use their legal training in their own brand of activism (Ginger, 1972).

Bibliography

Abel, E. (1982) *Writing and Sexual Difference* Chicago: University of Chicago Press.

Abel, R. ed. (1982a) *The Politics of Informal Justice*, Vol. I New York: Academic Press.

Abel, R. ed. (1982b) 'Torts' in D. Kairys ed. *The Politics of Law: A Progressive Critique* New York: Pantheon.

Abel, R. (1985) 'Comparative Sociology of Legal Professions: An Exploratory Essay' *American Bar Foundation Research Journal* 1.

Abel, R. (1988) 'United States: The Contradictions of Professionalism' in R. Abel and P. Lewis eds *Lawyers in Society* (*The Common Law World*) Berkeley: University of California Press.

Abel, R. and Lewis, P. eds (1988) *Lawyers in Society* (*The Common Law World*) Berkeley: University of California Press.

Adler, Z. (1987) *Rape on Trial* London: Routledge and Kegan Paul.

Allen, J. (1985) 'Desperately Seeking Solutions: Changing Battered Women's Options since 1880' in S. Hatty ed. *National Conference on Domestic Violence*, Vol. 1 Canberra: Australian Institute of Criminology.

Allen, J. (1987a) 'Policing Since 1880: Some Questions of Sex' in M. Finnane ed. *Policing in Australia: Historical Perspectives* Kensington: University of New South Wales Press.

Allen, J. (1987b) '"Mundane" Men: Historians, Masculinity and Masculinism' 22 *Historical Studies* 617.

Allen, J. (1988) 'The Masculinity of Criminality and Criminology: Interrogating Some Impasses' in M. Findlay and R. Hogg eds *Understanding Crime and Criminal Justice* Sydney: Law Book Company.

Allen, J. and Patton, P. eds (1983) *Beyond Marxism? Interventions After Marx* Sydney: Intervention Publications.

American Bar Association (ABA) (1988) Commission on Women in the Profession (Hillary Rodham Clinton, Chair) and Summary of Hearings, February.

Anon (1980) 'Lesbian Custody—A Personal Account' 20 *Refractory Girl* 2.

Aptheker, H. (1965) *A Documentary History of the Negro People in the United States* New York: Citadell Press.

Arthurs, H., Weisman, R. and Zemans, F. (1988) 'Canadian Lawyers: A Peculiar Professionalism' in R. Abel and P. Lewis eds *Lawyers in Society (The Common Law World)* Berkeley: University of California Press.

Attridge, I. and Bunting, A. et al. (1987) 'Gender in a Law School Classroom: Perceptions and Practices' unpublished manuscript, Osgoode Hall Law School, York University, Canada.

Austin, J. and Krisberg, B. (1981) 'Wider, Stronger and Different Nets: The Dialectics of Criminal Justice Reform' 18 *Journal of Research in Crime and Delinquency* 165.

Austin, R. (1986) 'Resistance Tactics for Tokens' 3 *Harvard Blackletter Law Journal* 52.

Australian Bureau of Statistics (ABS) (1986) *Census*.

Australian Bureau of Statistics (ABS) (1987) *Average Weekly Earnings*, May, Canberra: Australian Bureau of Statistics, Labour Force Catalogue No. 6203.3.

Australian Law Reform Commission (1986) *Transcript of Proceedings: Public Hearings on the Law of Contempt*.

Australian Law Reform Commission (1987a) *Contempt* Report No. 35 Canberra: AGPS.

Australian Law Reform Commission (1987b) *Matrimonial Property* Report No. 39 Canberra: AGPS.

Backhouse, C. (1985) '"To Open the Way for Others of my Sex": Clara Brett Martin's Career as Canada's First Woman Lawyer' 1 *Canadian Journal of Women and the Law* 1.

Baines, B. (1988) 'Women and the Law' in S. Burt, L. Code and L. Dorney eds *Changing Patterns: Women in Canada* Toronto: McClelland and Stewart.

Barblett, The Hon Mr Justice (1980) 'Custody of Children in Divorce, Separation and Similar Disputes: The Australian Experiment' 54 *Australian Law Journal* 489.

Bates, F. (1986) 'Australia: The Beginnings of a New Phase' 25 *Journal of Family Law* 3.

Bayefsky, A. and Eberts, M. eds (1987) *Equality Rights and the Canadian Charter of Rights and Freedoms* Toronto: Carswell.

Bell, D. (1985) 'The Supreme Court 1984 Term—Foreword: The Civil Rights Chronicles' 99 *Harvard Law Review* 1.

Benn, S.I. and Gaus, G.F. eds (1983) *Public and Private in Social Life* Canberra: Croom Helm.

Borowski, A. and Murray, J.M. eds (1985) *Juvenile Delinquency in Australia* Sydney: Methuen.

Bottomley, A.K. and Pease, K. (1986) *Crime and Punishment: Interpreting the Data* Philadelphia: Open University Press.

Bottoms, A.E. (1983) 'Neglected Features of Contemporary Penal Systems' in D. Garland and P. Young eds *The Power to Punish* London: Heinemann.

Boyd, S. (1987) 'Child Custody and Working Mothers' in K. Mahoney and S. Martin eds *Equality and Judicial Neutrality* Calgary: Carswell.

Boyd, S. (1989) 'Child Custody, Ideologies, and Employment' 3 *Canadian Journal of Women and the Law* 111.

Boyle, C. (1985) 'Book Review' 63 *Canadian Bar Review* 427.

Boyle, C. (1986) 'Teaching Law as if Women Really Mattered, or, What About the Washrooms?' 2 *Canadian Journal of Women and the Law* 96.

Bracamonte, J.A. (1987) 'Minority Critiques of the Critical Legal Studies Movement' 22 *Harvard Civil Rights—Civil Liberties Law Review* 297.

Brown, B. (1986) 'Women and Crime: The Dark Figures of Criminology' 15 *Economy and Society* 355.

Broom, D. ed. (1984) *Unfinished Business* Sydney: Allen and Unwin.

Bryson, L. (1985) 'Sharing the Caring: overcoming barriers to gender equality' 57 *Australian Quarterly* 300.

Burchell, G. (1981) 'Putting the Child in its Place' 8 *Ideology and Consciousness* 73.

Burnett, D. (1977) 'The Society's Computer' 11 *Law Society Gazette* 70.

Burt, S., Code, L. and Dorney, L. eds (1988) *Changing Patterns: Women in Canada* Toronto: McClelland and Stewart.

Cain, M. (1979) 'The General Practice Lawyer and the Client: Towards a Radical Conception' 7 *International Journal of the Sociology of Law* 331.

Cain, M. (1986) 'Socio-Legal Studies and Social Justice for Women: some Working Notes on a Method' paper presented at the Australian Law and Society Conference, Brisbane.

Campbell, A. (1981) *Girl Delinquents* Oxford: Basil Blackwell.

Campbell, B. (1980) 'A Feminist Sexual Politics: Now You See It, Now You Don't' 5 *Feminist Review* 1.

Canter, R.J. (1982) 'Family Correlates of Male and Female Delinquency' 20 *Criminology* 149.

Carlen, P. and Collinson, M. eds (1980) *Radical Issues in Criminology* Oxford: Martin Robinson.

Carlen, P. et al. (1985) *Criminal Women* Cambridge: Polity Press.

Chambers, G. and Millar, A. (1983) *Investigating Sexual Assault* Scottish Office, Edinburgh: HMSO.

Chesler, P. (1986) *Mothers on Trial: the Battle for Children and Custody* Seattle: Seal Press.

Chesney-Lind, M. (1977) 'Judicial Paternalism and the Female Status Offender: Training Women to Know Their Place' 23 *Crime and Delinquency* 121.

Child Welfare Practice and Legislation Review (CWPLR) (1985) *Report*, Vols I, II, III, Melbourne: Government Printer.

Chused, R.H. (1985) 'Faculty Parenthood: Law School Treatment of Pregnancy and Child Care' 35 *Journal of Legal Education* 568.

Clark, A. (1987) *Men's Violence: Women's Silence* London: Pandora.

Clark, L. and Lewis, D. (1977) *Rape: The Price of Coercive Sexuality* Toronto: The Women's Press.

Clarke, J. (1985) 'The Politics of Juvenile Control' 13 *International Journal of the Sociology of Law* 407.

Cohen, A.K. et al. eds (1956) *The Sutherland Papers* Bloomington: Indiana University Press.

Cohen, A.K. (1955) *Delinquent Boys New York*: The Free Press.

Cohen, S. (1979) 'The Punitive City: Notes on the Dispersal of Social Control' 3 *Contemporary Crises* 339.

Cohen, S. (1983) 'Social-Control Talk: Telling Stories about Correctional Change' in D. Garland and P. Young eds *The Power to Punish* London: Heinemann.

Cohen, S. (1985) *Visions of Social Control* Cambridge: Polity Press.

Cohen, S. and Reddon, A. (1988) 'The Impact of Feminists at Queen's Law School: 1985–1988' unpublished manuscript, Queen's University.

Collison, M. (1980) 'Questions of Juvenile Justice' in P. Carlen and M. Collison eds *Radical Issues in Criminology* Oxford: Martin Robinson.

Community Services Victoria (May 1986) *Discussion Paper on Redevelopment of Services for Children and Young People in Allambie, Baltara and Winlaton.*

Community Services Victoria (October 1986) *Discussion Paper on Redevelopment of Services for Young People Convicted of Committing Offences.*

Community Services Victoria (1987) *Draft Strategy Plan: Implementation Plan for the Redevelopment of CSV Protective and Correctional Services for Young People.*

Cook, R. and Mitchinson, W. eds (1976) *The Proper Sphere: Woman's Place in Canadian Society* Toronto: Oxford University Press.

Cott, N. (1979) 'Passionlessness: An Interpretation of Victorian Sexual Ideology, 1790–1850' 4 *Signs* 219.

Cousins, M. (1980) 'Men's Rea: A Note on Sexual Difference, Criminology and the Law' in P. Carlen and M. Collison eds *Radical Issues in Criminology* Oxford: Martin Robertson.

Cousins, M. and Hussain, A. (1984) *Michel Foucault* London: Macmillan.

Couzens Hoy, D. ed. (1986) *Foucault: A Critical Reader* Oxford: Blackwell.

Crites, L. ed. (1976) *The Female Offender* Lexington, Massachusetts: Lexington Books.

Dalton, H.L. (1987) 'The Clouded Prism' 22 *Harvard Civil Rights—Civil Liberties Law Review* 435.

Davis, J. (1983) *The First-Born and Other Poems* Sydney: Angus and Robertson.

Davis, P.C. (1987) '"There is a Book Out . . . ": An Analysis of Judicial Absorption of Legislative Facts' 100 *Harvard Law Review* 1539.

Delgado, R. (1984) 'The Imperial Scholar: Reflections on a Review of Civil Rights Literature' 132 *University of Pennsylvania Law Review* 561.

Delgado, R. (1987) 'The Ethereal Scholar: Does Critical Legal Studies Have What Minorities Want?' 22 *Harvard Civil Rights—Civil Liberties Law Review* 301.

Department of Social Security (1988) *Annual Report: 1987–1988* Canberra: AGPS.

Diamond, A. and Edwards, L. eds (1977) *The Authority of Experience: Essays in Feminist Criticism* Amherst, Massachusetts: University of Massachusetts Press.

Dickey, A. (1985) *Family Law* Sydney: Law Book Co.

Dubois, E., Dunlap, M., Gilligan, C., MacKinnon, C., Menkel-Meadow, C. (1985) 'Feminist Discourse, Moral Values and the Law—A Conversation' 34 *Buffalo Law Review* 11.

Duchen, C. (1986) *Feminism in France* London: Routledge and Kegan Paul.

Edgar, D. (1986) 'Marriage, the Family and Family Law in Australia' Discussion Paper No. 13, Melbourne: Australian Institute of Family Studies.

Edley, C. (1986) 'Affirmative Action and the Rights Rhetoric Trap' in R.K. Fullinwider and C. Mills eds *The Moral Foundations of Civil Rights* Totowa, New Jersey: Rowman and Littlefield.

Ellis, W. (1901) *The Criminal* London: Walter Scott.

Empey, L.T. (1978) *American Delinquency: Its Meaning and Constructions* Homewood Illinois: Dorsey Press.

Empey, L.T. (1980) 'Revolution and Counter-revolution: Current Trends in Juvenile Justice' in D. Shichor and D. H. Kelly eds *Critical Issues in Juvenile Delinquency* Lexington, Massachusetts: Lexington Books.

Family Law Council (1987) *Access—Some Options for Reform* Canberra: AGPS.

Felstiner, W.L.F., Abel, R. and Sarat, A. (1981) 'The Emergence and Transformation of Disputes: Naming, Blaming, Claiming' 15 *Law and Society Review* 631.

Feminist Anti-Censorship Taskforce (FACT) (1987–8) '*Amicus Curiae* brief in *Hudnut*' 21 *University of Michigan Journal of Law Reform* 69.

Fiedler, A. and Hart, C.D. (1986) 'Stratospheric Aerosols: The Transfer of Scientific Information' 8 *Library and Information Science Research* 243.

Figueira-McDonough, J. and Selo, E. (1980) 'A Reformulation of the "Equal Opportunity" Explanation of Female Delinquency' 26 *Crime and Delinquency* 333.

Figueira-McDonough, J. (1987) 'Discrimination of Sex Differences: Criteria for Evaluating the Juvenile Justice System's Handling of Minor Offences' 33 *Crime and Delinquency* 403.

Findlay, M. and Hogg, R. eds (1988) *Understanding Crime and Criminal Justice* Sydney: Law Book Company.

Fineman, M. (1983) 'Implementing Equality: Ideology, Contradiction and Social Change. A Study of Rhetoric and Results in the Regulation of the Consequences of Divorce' *Wisconsin Law Review* 789.

Fineman, M. (1986) 'Illusive Equality: On Weitzman's *Divorce Revolution*' *American Bar Foundation Research Journal* 781.

Fineman, M. (1988) 'Dominant Discourse, Professional Language and Legal Change—Child Custody Decisionmaking' 101 *Harvard Law Review* 727.

Finlay, H.A. (1983) *Family Law in Australia* Sydney: Butterworths.

Finnane, M. ed. (1987) *Policing in Australia: Historical Perspectives* Kensington: University of New South Wales Press.

Fitzroy Legal Service (1986) *A 'Yes Minister' Approach to De-Institutionalisation*.

Foucault, M. (1977) *Discipline and Punish* London: Penguin.

Foucault, M. (1979) 'An Introduction' in *History of Sexuality*, Vol. 1 London: Penguin.

Foucault, M. (1980) 'Two Lectures' in C. Gordon ed. *Michel Foucault: Power/Knowledge: Selected Interviews and other Writings 1972–1977* Brighton: Harvester Press.

Freiberg, A. (1987) 'Reconceptualizing Sanctions' 25 *Criminology* 223.

Freiberg, A. (1988) 'The State as a Victim of Crime' 21 *Australian and New Zealand Journal of Criminology* 20.

Friedman, L.M. and Ladinsky, J. (1967) 'Social Change and the Law of Industrial Accidents' 67 *Columbia Law Review* 50.

Fuchs Epstein, C. (1981) 'Women and Elites: A Cross-National Perspective' in C. Fuchs Epstein and R. Laub Coser eds *Access to Power: Cross-National Studies of Women and Elites* London: Allen and Unwin.

Fuchs Epstein, C. and Laub Coser, R. eds (1981) *Access to Power: Cross-National Studies of Women and Elites* London: Allen and Unwin.

Fullinwider, R.K. and Mills, C. eds (1986) *The Moral Foundations of Civil Rights* Totowa, New Jersey: Rowman and Littlefield.

Gamble, H. (1985) 'The Status Offender' in A. Borowski and J.M. Murray eds *Juvenile Delinquency in Australia* Sydney: Methuen.

Game, A. and Pringle, R. (1984) 'Production and Consumption' in D. Broom ed. *Unfinished Business* Sydney: Allen and Unwin.

Garland, D. and Young, P. eds (1983) *The Power to Punish* London: Heinemann.

Gatens, M. (1983) 'A Critique of the Sex/Gender Distinction' in J. Allen and P. Patton eds *Beyond Marxism? Interventions After Marx* Sydney: Intervention Publications.

Gillet, M. (1981) *We Walked Very Warily: A History of Women at McGill* Montreal: Black Rose Books.

Gilligan, C. (1982) *In a Different Voice* Cambridge, Massachusetts: Harvard University Press.

Ginger, A.F. (1972) *Relevant Lawyers: Conversations Out of Court on Their Clients, Their Practice, Their Politics, Their Lifestyle* New York: Simon and Schuster.

Gordon, C. ed. (1980) *Michel Foucault: Power/Knowledge: Selected Interviews and Other Writings 1972–1977* Brighton: Harvester Press.

Gordon, R. (1984) 'Critical Legal Studies Symposium: Critical Legal Histories' 36 *Stanford Law Review* 57.

Gould, M. and Kern-Daniels, R. (1977) 'Toward a Sociological Theory of Gender and Sex' 12 *American Sociologist* 182.

Graycar, R. (1985a) 'Compensation for Loss of Capacity to Work in the Home' 10 *Sydney Law Review* 528.

Graycar, R. (1985b) 'Hoovering as a Hobby: the Common Law's Approach to Work in the Home' 28 *Refractory Girl* 22.

Graycar, R. (1988) 'Violence in the Home: A Legal Response—A Limited Solution?' 26 *Law Society Journal* 46 (May).

Graycar, R. (1989a) 'Family Law and Social Security: The Child Support Connection' 3 *Australian Journal of Family Law* 70.

Graycar, R. (1989b) 'Equal Rights versus Fathers' Rights: The Child Custody Debate in Australia' in C. Smart and S. Sevenhuijsen eds *Child Custody and the Politics of Gender* London: Routledge.

Graycar, R. and Shiff, D. eds (1987) *Life Without Marriage: A Woman's Guide to the Law* Sydney: Pluto Press.

Graycar, R. and Morgan, J. (forthcoming 1990) *The Hidden Gender of Law* Sydney: Federation Press.

Greenwood, J. (1981) 'The Myth of Female Crime' in A. Morris and L.

Gelsthorpe eds *Women and Crime* Cambridge: Cambridge Institute of Criminology.

Gregory, J. (1988) *Sex, Race and the Law* London: Sage.

Gross, E. (1986) 'Philosophy, Subjectivity and the Body: Kristeva and Irigaray' in C. Pateman and E. Gross eds *Feminist Challenges: Social and Political Theory* Sydney: Allen and Unwin.

Grosz, E. (1987a) 'Feminism and Social Theory' unpublished paper, presented to the Department of Anthropology and Sociology, University of Queensland 30 October.

Grosz, E. (1987b) 'Notes Towards a Corporeal Feminism' 5 *Australian Feminist Studies* 1.

Guthrie, B. and Kingshott, M. (1987) 'Children', in R. Graycar and D. Shiff eds *Life Without Marriage: A Woman's Guide to the Law* Sydney: Pluto Press.

Hall, R. and Sandler, B. (1982) *The Classroom Climate: A Chilly One for Women?* Washington D.C: Project on the Status and Education of Women.

Hancock, L. and Chesney-Lind, M. (1985) 'Juvenile Justice Legislation and Gender Discrimination' in A. Borowski and J.M. Murray eds *Juvenile Delinquency in Australia* Sydney: Methuen.

Harding, S. (1986) *The Science Question in Feminism* Milton Keynes: Open University Press.

Harding, S. ed. (1987) *Feminism and Methodology* Bloomington: Indiana University Press.

Harris, A. (1977) 'Sex and Theories of Deviance' 42 *American Sociological Review* 3.

Harris, R. (1987) 'The Flowering of Afro-American History' 92 *American Historical Review* 1150.

Harvey, C. (1970) 'Women in Law in Canada' 4 *Manitoba Law Journal* 9.

Hatty, S. ed. (1985) *National Conference on Domestic Violence*, Vol. 1 Canberra: Australian Institute of Criminology.

Haug, F. ed. (1987) *Female Sexualisation* London: Verso.

Heidensohn, F.M. (1968) 'The Deviance of Women: A Critique and an Enquiry' 19 *British Journal of Sociology* 160.

Heidensohn, F.M. (1985) *Women and Crime* London: Macmillan.

Hellum, F. (1979) 'Juvenile Justice: The Second Revolution' 25 *Crime and Delinquency* 299.

Henderson, G. (1929) 'Eligibility of Women for the Senate' 7 *Canadian Bar Review* 617.

Heron, A. (1987) 'Child Support: Making Fathers Pay' 12 *Legal Service Bulletin* 17.

Hindelang, M. (1979) 'Sex Differences in Criminal Activity' 27 *Social Problems* 143.

Hogg, R. and Brown, D. (1985) 'Reforming Juvenile Justice: Issues and Prospects' in A. Borowski and J.M. Murray eds *Juvenile Justice in Australia* Sydney: Methuen.

hooks, b. (1981) *Ain't I a Woman: Black Women and Feminism* Boston: South End Press.

Horwill, F. and Bordow, S. (1983) *The Outcome of Defended Custody*

Cases in the Family Court of Australia Research Report No.4 Sydney: Family Court of Australia.

Howe, A. (1987a) '"Social Injury" Revisited: Towards a Feminist Theory of Social Justice' 15 *International Journal of the Sociology of Law* 423.

Howe, A. (1987b) 'The Problem of Privatized Injuries: Feminist Strategies for Litigation' paper presented at the Feminism and Legal Theory Conference University of Wisconsin Law School, Madison, Wisconsin.

Howe, B. (1987) 'Reforms to Child Support' Ministerial Statement to Parliament, House of Representatives Parliamentary Debates, 24 March, p.1368.

Hull, G. (1984) *Give Us Each Day: Diary of Alice Dunbar-Nelson* New York: W.W. Norton.

Huntington, J.F. (1982) 'Powerless and Vulnerable: The Social Experience of Imprisoned Girls' 33 *Juvenile and Family Court Journal* 33.

Jensen, G.J. and Raymond, D. (1976) 'Sex Differences in Delinquency: An Examination of Popular Sociological Explanations' 13 *Criminology* 427.

Jessep, O. and Chisholm, R. (1985) 'Children, the Constitution and the Family Court' 8 *University of New South Wales Law Journal* 152.

Johnson, C. (1986) *The Song Circle of Jacky and Selected Poems* Melbourne: Hyland House.

Jordan, J. (1986) 'Cultural Nationalism in the 1960s: Politics and Poetry' in A. Reed ed. *Race, Politics, and Culture: Critical Essays on the Radicalism of the 1960s* Westport, Connecticut: Greenwood Press.

Kairys, D. ed. (1982) *The Politics of Law: A Progressive Critique* New York: Pantheon.

Kelly, L. (1989) *Surviving Sexual Assault* Cambridge: Polity.

Kennedy, D. (1983) *Legal Education and the Reproduction of Hierarchy: A Polemic Against the System* Cambridge: Afar.

Kinsey, A. et al. (1949) *Sexual Behaviour in the Human Male* Philadelphia: W.B. Saunders.

Kinsey, A. (1953) *Sexual Behaviour in the Human Female* Philadelphia: W.B. Saunders.

Kitano, H. (1980) *Race Relations* 2nd ed. Englewood Cliffs, N.J: Prentice-Hall.

Klein, D. (1976) 'The Aetiology of Female Crime: A Review of the Literature' 8 *Crime and Social Justice* 3.

Klein, M. (1979) 'Deinstitutionalisation and Diversion: A Litany of Impediments' in N. Morris and M. Tonry eds *Crime and Justice: An Annual Review of Research*, Vol. 1 Chicago: University of Chicago Press.

Kliger, B. (1988) 'The Child Support Scheme: Who is Reaping the Benefits?' 13 *Legal Service Bulletin* 16.

Koedt, A. (1970) 'The Myth of the Vaginal Orgasm' in L. Tanner ed. *Voices from Women's Liberation* New York: Signet.

Krisberg, B. and Schwartz, I. (1983) 'Rethinking Juvenile Justice' 29 *Crime and Delinquency* 333.

Krisberg, B. et al. (1986) 'The Watershed of Juvenile Justice Reform' 32 Crime and Delinquency 5.

Krupnick, C. (1985) 'Women and Men in the Classroom: Inequality and its

Remedies' *On Teaching and Learning* (Journal of the Harvard-Danforth Centre) 18.

Kuhn, A. (1985) *The Power of the Image* London: Routledge and Kegan Paul.

Kuhn, T. (1970) *The Structure of Scientific Revolutions* Chicago: University of Chicago Press.

Kvaraceus, W.C. and Miller, W.B. (1959) *Delinquent Behaviour: Culture and the Individual* Washington, D.C: Juvenile Delinquency Project, National Education Association of the US.

Lahey, K. (1985) '. . . until women themselves have told all that they have to tell . . .' 23 *Osgoode Hall Law Journal* 519.

Lake, M. (1986) 'The Politics of Respectability: Identifying the Masculinist Context' 22 *Historical Studies* 116.

Lawrence, C.R.C. (1986) 'Minority Hiring in AALS Law Schools: The Need for Voluntary Quotas' 20 *University of San Francisco Law Review* 429.

Lees, S. (1986) *Sexuality and Adolescent Girls* London: Hutchinson.

Lehmann, G. (1983) 'The Case For Joint Custody' *Quadrant*, June, p. 60.

Lemert, E. (1981) 'Diversion: What Hath Been Wrought' 18 *Journal of Research in Crime and Delinquency* 34.

Leonard, E.B. (1982) *Women, Crime and Society: A Critique of Criminological Theory* New York: Longmans.

Lerman, P. (1984) 'Child Welfare, the Private Sector, and Community-Based Correction' 30 *Crime and Delinquency* 5.

Lerner, G. (1986) *The Creation of Patriarchy* New York: Oxford University Press.

Lombroso, C. and Ferraro, W. (1895) *The Female Offender* London: Fisher Unwin.

Lorde, A. (1984) *Sister Outsider: Essays and Speeches* Trumansburg, New York: Crossing Press.

Lovell Banks, T. (1988) 'Gender Bias in the Classroom' 38 *Journal of Legal Education* 137.

Mackinolty, J. and Radi, H. eds (1979) *In Pursuit of Justice: Australian Women and the Law 1788–1979* Sydney: Hale and Iremonger.

MacKinnon, C.A. (1979) *Sexual Harassment of Working Women: A Case of Sex Discrimination* New Haven: Yale University Press.

MacKinnon, C.A. (1983) 'Feminism, Marxism, Method and the State: Toward Feminist Jurisprudence' 8 *Signs* 635.

MacKinnon, C.A. (1985a) Dubois, E. et al. (1985) 'Feminist Discourse, Moral Values and the Law—A Conversation' 34 *Buffalo Law Review* 11.

MacKinnon, C.A. (1985b) 'Pornography, Civil Rights, and Speech' 20 *Harvard Civil Rights—Civil Liberties Law Review* 1.

MacKinnon, C.A. (1987) *Feminism Unmodified: Discourses on Life and Law* Cambridge MA: Harvard University Press.

MacKinnon, C.A. (1989) *Toward a Feminist Theory of the State* Cambridge MA: Harvard University Press.

Mahoney, K. and Martin, S. eds (1987) *Equality and Judicial Neutrality* Calgary: Carswell.

Martin, D. (1984) *The Mind of Frederick Douglass* Chapel Hill: University of North Carolina Press.

Matsuda, M. (1986) 'Liberal Jurisprudence and Abstracted Visions of Human Nature: A Feminist Critique of Rawls' Theory of Justice' 16 *New Mexico Law Review* 613.

Matsuda, M. (1987) 'Looking to the Bottom: Critical Legal Studies and Reparations' 22 *Harvard Civil Rights—Civil Liberties Law Review* 323.

Matsuda, M. (1988) 'Affirmative Action and Legal Knowledge: Planting Seeds in Plowed-Up Ground' 11 *Harvard Women's Law Journal* 1.

Matthews, R. (1987) 'Decarceration and Social Control: Fantasies and Realities' 15 *International Journal of the Sociology of Law* 39.

McDonald, P.J. ed. and The Australian Institute of Family Studies (1986) *Settling up: Property and Income Distribution on Divorce in Australia* Melbourne: Prentice Hall.

McMillen, L. (1987) 'Universities are Lagging in Hiring Women and Blacks for Faculty Jobs 2 Studies Find' *The Chronicle of Higher Education*, July 8, 11.

McRobbie, A. and Nava, M. eds (1984) *Gender and Generation*, London: Macmillan.

Mead, M. (1935) *Sex and Temperament in Three Primitive Societies* New York: Morrow.

Men's Confraternity (n.d.—1985 ?) Submission to the Australian Law Reform Commission Inquiry on Matrimonial Property, on file, Australian Law Reform Commission.

Menkel-Meadow, C. (1987) 'Excluded Voices: New Voices in the Legal Profession Making New Voices in the Law' 42 *University of Miami Law Review* 29.

Menkel-Meadow, C. (1988) 'Feminist Legal Theory, Critical Legal Studies, and Legal Education or "The Fem-Crits Go to Law School"' 38 *Journal of Legal Education* 61.

Miller, J.B. (1976) *Toward a New Psychology of Women* Boston: Beacon Press.

Miller, W.B. (1958) 'Lower Class Culture as a Generating Milieu of Gang Delinquency' 14 *Journal of Social Issues* 5.

Minow, M. (1987) 'Justice Engendered' 101 *Harvard Law Review* 10.

Minow, M. (1988) 'Feminist Reason: Getting It and Losing It' 38 *Journal of Legal Education* 47.

Mitra, C.L. (1987) 'Judicial Discourse in Father-Daughter Incest Appeal Cases' 15 *International Journal of the Sociology of Law* 121.

Morash, M. (1986) 'Gender, Peer Group Experiences and Seriousness of Delinquency' 23 *Journal of Research in Crime and Delinquency* 43.

Morgan, J. (1989) 'The Socratic Method: Silencing Cooperation' 1 *Legal Education Review* 151.

Morgentaler, G. (1984) 'McGill Alumnae Through the Decades: Part II' *McGill News* (Fall) 18.

Morris, A. and Gelsthorpe, L. eds (1981) *Women and Crime* Cambridge: Cambridge Institute of Criminology.

Morris, N. and Tonry, M. eds (1979) *Crime and Justice: An Annual Review of Research*, Vol. 1 Chicago: University of Chicago Press.

Moss Kanter, R. (1977) *Men and Women of the Corporation* New York: Basic Books.

Moss Kanter, R. (1978) 'Reflections on Women and the Legal Profession: A Sociological Perspective' 1 *Harvard Women's Law Journal* 1.

Mossman, M.J. (1986) 'Feminism and Legal Method—The Difference it Makes' 3 *Australian Journal of Law and Society* 30.

Mossman, M.J. (1987) 'Feminism and Legal Method—The Difference it Makes' 3 *Wisconsin Women's Law Journal* 147.

Mossman, M.J. (1988) '"Invisible" Constraints on Lawyering and Leadership: The Case of Women Lawyers' 20 *Ottawa Law Review* 567.

Mullins, C. (1986) 'Mabel Penury French' 44 *The Advocate* 676.

Murch, M. et al. (1987) *Overlapping Family Jurisdiction of Magistrates' Courts and County Courts* Research Report, London: Lord Chancellor's Department.

Murray, G. (1988) 'New Zealand Lawyers: From Colonial GP's to the Servants of Capital' in R. Abel and P. Lewis eds *Lawyers in Society (The Common Law World)* Berkeley: University of California Press.

Nava, M. (1984) 'Youth Service Provision, Social Order and the Question of Girls' in A. McRobbie and M. Nava eds *Gender and Generation* London: MacMillan.

O'Brien, M. and McIntyre, S. (1986) 'Patriarchal Hegemony and Legal Education' 2 *Canadian Journal of Women and the Law* 69.

O'Donovan, K. (1985) *Sexual Divisions in Law* Weidenfeld and Nicolson: London.

Parsons, T. (1942) 'Age and Sex in the Social Structure of the United States' 7 *American Sociological Review* 604.

Parsons, T. (1951) *The Social System* New York: Macmillan.

Pateman, C. (1983) 'Feminist Critiques of the Public/Private Dichotomy' in S.I. Benn and G.F. Gaus eds *Public and Private in Social Life* Canberra: Croom Helm.

Pateman, C. and Gross, E. eds (1986) *Feminist Challenges: Social and Political Theory* Sydney: Allen and Unwin.

Patullo, P. (1983) *Judging Women* London: National Council for Civil Liberties.

Pazdro, R. (1980) 'Of British Columbia Suffragists and Barristers' 2 (4) *Canadian Women's Studies* 15.

Pickard, T. (1986) 'Is Real Life Finally Happening?' 2 *Canadian Journal of Women and the Law* 150.

Prisoners Action Group (1980) Submission to the Royal Commission into NSW Prisons 3 *Alternative Criminology Journal* 1.

Radi, H. (1979) 'Whose Child?' in J. Mackinolty and H. Radi eds *In Pursuit of Justice: Australian Women and the Law 1788–1979* Sydney: Hale and Iremonger.

Rampersad, A. (1986) *The Life of Langston Hughes* New York: Oxford University Press.

Rathjen, G. (1976) 'The Impact of Legal Education on the Beliefs, Attitudes and Values of Law Students' 44 *Tennesee Law Journal* 83.

Ravitch, D. and Finn, C. (1987) *What Do Our 17-Year-Olds Know: A*

Report on the First National Assessment of History and Literature New York: Harper and Row.

Reed, A. ed. (1986) *Race, Politics and Culture: Critical Essays on the Radicalism of the 1960s* Westport, Connecticut: Greenwood Press.

Riddell, W. (1918) 'Women as Practitioners of Law' 18 *Journal of Society of Comparative Legislation* 200.

Rifkin, J. (1980) 'Toward a Theory of Law and Patriarchy' 3 *Harvard Women's Law Journal* 83.

Robert, E.R. and Winter, M.F. (1978) 'Sex-Role and Success in Law School' 29 *Journal of Legal Education* 449.

Ronalds, C. (1987) *Affirmative Action and Sex Discrimination: A Handbook on Legal Rights for Women* Sydney: Pluto Press.

Rosenblum, K. (1975) 'Female Deviance and the Female Sex Role: A Preliminary Investigation' 25 *British Journal of Sociology* 169.

Russell, G. (1983) *The Changing Role of Fathers?* St Lucia: University of Queensland Press.

Sachs, A. and Hoff Wilson, J. (1978) *Sexism and the Law: A Study of Male Beliefs and Legal Bias in Britain and the United States* London: Martin Robertson.

Samuels, Justice Gordon (1982) comments reproduced in *Assessment of Damages* Committee for Post-Graduate Studies in the Department of Law, Sydney University, November.

Sarri, R.C. (1976) 'Juvenile Law: How it Penalises Females' in L. Crites ed. *The Female Offender* Lexington, Massachusetts: Lexington Books.

Sarri, R.C. (1983) 'Gender Issues in Juvenile Justice' 29 *Crime and Delinquency* 381.

Schlossman, S. and Wallach, S. (1978) 'The Crime of Precocious Sexuality: Female Juvenile Delinquency in the Progressive Era' 48 *Harvard Educational Review* 65.

Schneider, E. (1988) 'Task Force Reports on Women in the Courts: the Challenge for Legal Education' 38 *Journal of Legal Education* 87.

Schulman, J. and Pitt, V. (1982) 'Second Thoughts on Joint Child Custody: Analysis of Legislation and its Implications for Women and Children' 12 *Golden Gate University Law Review* 538.

Scutt, J. (1976) 'Role Conditioning Theory: An Explanation for the Disparity in Male and Female Criminality?' 9 *Australian and New Zealand Journal of Criminology* 1.

Scutt, J. (1983) 'Equal Marital Property Rights' 18 *Australian Journal of Social Issues* 128.

Scutt, J. and Graham, D. (1984) *For Richer, For Poorer* Melbourne: Penguin.

Sevenhuijsen, S. (1986) 'Fatherhood and the Political Theory of Rights: Theoretical Perspectives of Feminism' 14 *International Journal of the Sociology of Law* 329.

Shichor, D. and Kelly, D.H. eds (1980) *Critical Issues in Juvenile Delinquency* Lexington, Massachusetts: Lexington Books.

Shiff, D. and McIllhatton, S. (1985) 'Review of *For Richer, For Poorer*' 11 *Legal Service Bulletin* 29.

123

Shorts, I.D. (1986) 'In-Programme Failure among Delinquent Youths in Community-Based Programmes: Some Reflections on a Neglected Area of Research' 30 *International Journal of Offender Therapy and Comparative Criminology* 245.

Silverman, I.R. and Sinitz, D. (1974) 'Compulsive Masculinity and Delinquency: an empirical investigation' 11 *Criminology* 498.

Smart, B. (1983) 'On Discipline and Social Regulation: a Review of Foucault's Genealogical Analysis' in D. Garland and P. Young eds *The Power to Punish* London: Heinemann.

Smart, B. (1985) *Michel Foucault* London: Tavistock.

Smart, C. (1976) *Women, Crime and Criminology: A Feminist Critique* London: Routledge and Kegan Paul.

Smart, C. (1984) *The Ties That Bind* London: Routledge and Kegan Paul.

Smart, C. (1986) 'Feminism and Law: Some Problems of Analysis and Strategy' 14 *International Journal of the Sociology of Law* 109.

Smart, C. (1989a) 'The Politics of Child Custody: an Introduction' in C. Smart and S. Sevenhuijsen eds *Child Custody and the Politics of Gender* London: Routledge.

Smart, C. (1989b) *Feminism and the Power of Law* London: Routledge.

Smart, C. and Sevenhuijen, S. eds (1989) *Child Custody and the Politics of Gender* London: Routledge.

Smart, C. and Smart, B. (1978) *Women, Sexuality and Social Control* London: Routledge and Kegan Paul.

Smith, D. and Paternoster, R. (1987) 'The Gender Gap in Theories of Deviance: Issues and Evidence' 24 *Journal of Research in Crime and Delinquency* 140.

Stang Dahl, T. and Snare, A. (1978) 'The Coercion of Privacy: A Feminist Perspective' in C. Smart and B. Smart eds *Women, Sexuality and Social Control* London: Routledge and Kegan Paul.

Stang Dahl, T. (1986) 'Taking Women as a Starting Point: Building Women's Law' 14 *International Journal of the Sociology of Law* 239.

Stang Dahl, T. (1987) *Women's Law: An Introduction to Feminist Jurisprudence* Oxford: Oxford University Press.

Sutherland, E. (1945) 'Is "White-collar Crime" Crime?' 10 *American Sociological Review* 132.

Tanner, L. ed. (1970) *Voices From Women's Liberation* New York: Signet.

Tappan, P. (1947) 'Who is the Criminal?' 12 *American Sociological Review* 96.

Taylor, C. (1986) 'Foucault on Freedom and Truth' in D. Couzens Hoy ed. *Foucault: A Critical Reader* Oxford: Blackwell.

Taylor, L., Lacey, R. and Bracken, D. (1979) *In Whose Best Interests?* London: Mind/Cobden Trust.

Thomas, W.I. (1907) *Sex and Society* Boston: Little Brown.

Thomas, W.I. (1923) *The Unadjusted Girl* New York: Repr. Harper and Row, 1967.

Thornton, W.E. and James, J. (1979) 'Masculinity and Delinquency Revisited' 19 *British Journal of Criminology* 225.

Torres, G. and Brewster, D.P. (1986) 'Judges and Juries: Separate Moments in the Same Phenomenon' 4 *Law and Inequality: A Journal of Theory and Practice* 171.

Treichler, P., Kramarae, C. and Stafford, B. eds (1985) *For Alma Mater: Theory and Practice in Feminist Scholarship* Urbana: University of Illinois Press.

Trubek, D. (1981) 'The Construction and De-construction of a Disputes-focused Approach: an Afterword' 15 *Law and Society Review* 727.

Walker, A. (1985) 'On Excellence: America Should Have Closed Down on the First Day a Black Woman Observed That Supermarket Collard Greens Tasted like Water' *MS*, January: 53.

Walker, K. (1970) *My People* Milton, Queensland: Jacaranda.

Ward, E. (1984) *Father-Daughter Rape* London: The Women's Press.

Watson, S. (1986) *Housing and Homelessness: A Feminist Perspective* London: Routledge and Kegan Paul.

Watson, S. (1988) *Accommodating Inequality: Gender and Housing* Sydney: Allen and Unwin.

Watson, S. and Coleman, L. (1986) 'Housing Demographic Change and the Private Rental Sector' 21 *Australian Journal of Social Issues* 16.

Watson, S. and Shiff, D. (1984) 'Divorce's Real Cost: The Unequal End to Marriage' 3 (8) *Australian Society* 17.

Watts, A. (1984) *History of the Legal Profession in British Columbia (1869–1984)* Vancouver: Law Society of British Columbia.

Webb, S. and Nelson, R.W. (1980) *Selma, Lord, Selma: Girlhood Memories of the Civil Rights Days* New York: Morrow.

Weedon, C. (1987) *Feminist Practice and Poststructuralist Theory* Oxford: Blackwell.

Weisberg, D.K. (1982) 'Barred from the Bar: Women and Legal Education in the United States, 1870–1890' in D.K. Weisberg ed. *Women and the Law*, Vol. 2 Cambridge, MA: Shenkman.

Weisberg, D.K. ed. (1982) *Women and the Law*, Vol. 2 Cambridge, MA: Shenkman.

Weisbrot, D. (1988) 'The Australian Legal Profession: From Provincial Family Firms to Multinationals' in R. Abel and P. Lewis eds *Lawyers in Society (The Common Law World)* Berkeley: University of California Press.

Weiss, C. and Melling, L. (1988) 'The Legal Education of Twenty Women' 40 *Stanford Law Review* 1299.

Weitzman, L. (1985) *The Divorce Revolution: The Unexpected Social and Economic Consequences for Women and Children in America* New York: Free Press.

Weller, A. (1986) *Going Home* Sydney: Allen and Unwin.

West, R. (1987) 'The Difference in Women's Hedonic Lives: a Phenomenological Critique of Feminist Legal Theory' 3 *Wisconsin Women's Law Journal* 81.

Williams, P.J. (1987) 'Alchemical Notes: Reconstructing Ideals from Reconstructed Rights' 22 *Harvard Civil Rights—Civil Liberties Law Review* 401.

Williams, R.A. (1986) 'The Algebra of Federal Indian Law: The Hard Trial of Decolonizing and Americanizing the White Man's Indian Jurisprudence' *Wisconsin Law Review* 219.

Winlaton (1987) *Manual of Guidelines and Procedures.*

Women's Bureau, Department of Employment, Education and Training (1988) *Women's Work, Women's Pay: Industrial and Occupational Segregation of Women in the Workforce* Canberra: DEET.

Women's Coordination Unit (1986) *Girls at Risk* Sydney: Premier's Department, NSW.

Worden, K.C. (1986) 'A Student Polemic' 16 *New Mexico Law Review* 573.

Youth Accommodation Coalition of Victoria (YAC) (1986) *Deinstitutionalisation: A Community-Based Perspective.*

Cases

AUSTRALIA

Epperson v *Dampney* (1976) 10 ALR 227
Gronow v *Gronow* (1979) 144 CLR 513
Harrington v *Hynes* (1982) 8 Fam LR 295
Mathieson and Mathieson (1977) FLC 90-230
Swaney v *Ward* (1988) FLC 91-928
W v *W* No. AD1039 of 1985, Family Court of Australia, Adelaide, 6 August, 7 October 1987 (unreported)

CANADA

In re French (1906) 37 NBR 359
Re French (1910–1912) 17 BCLR 1 (1911)
Re French (1910–1912) 17 BCLR 4 (1912)
Langstaff v *Bar of Quebec* (1915) 47 R.Jud. Que. 131
Langstaff v *Bar of Quebec* (1916) 25 R.Jud. Que. 11 (Cours du Ban du Roi)

UNITED KINGDOM

Bebb v *Law Society* (1913) 29 TLR 634; aff'd (1914) 30 TLR 179 (C.A.)
Edwards v *Attorney-General for Canada* [1930] AC 124
Hall v *Incorp. Society of Law Agents* 3 Session Cases, 5th series 1059 (1901)

UNITED STATES

Bradwell v *Illinois* 21 L.Ed. 442 (1873)

Statutes

AUSTRALIA

Family Law Act 1975 (Cth)
Sex Discrimination Act 1984 (Cth)

CANADA

New Brunswick

Act to Remove the Disability of Women so far as relates to the Study and
Practice of Law, 6 Ed. VII, c.5 (1906)
Barristers' Society Act, C.S.N.B., c.68 (1903)

Ontario

Act to Provide for the Admission of Women to the Study and Practice of
Law, 55 Vic., c.32 (1892); and 58 Vic., c.27 (1895)

British Columbia

Act to Remove the Disability of Women so far as relates to the Study and
Practice of Law, 2 Geo. V, c.18 (1912)
Legal Professions Act, R.S.B.C. 1897, c.24

Quebec

Liberal Professions Act, R.S.Q. 1909, c.2

Index